The Microwave Cookbook

The Ultimate Microwave Cookbook Guide for Busy Days with Over 100 Recipes for Easy, Quick and Delicious Meals for Beginners.

Jessica Smith

Contents

What Kinds of Microwave Ovens Are There?

When selecting the ideal microwave oven, we are frequently faced with a conundrum. This is due to the wide variety of options available. Both their appearance and their functions are different. It is simple to choose one that would fit comfortably within your budget based on the requirements you have in your kitchen. Keep in mind that microwaves are an investment, therefore it is worthwhile to spend a little more to acquire the highest quality. This will also guarantee its long-term durability. Here are some examples of several microwave oven models.

Oven with convection

Convection is used in this oven to heat the food inside. The hot air cooks and crusts everything evenly thanks to a fan and heating elements.

Grill Oven

Kebabs, meats, and tikkas, which are known for being crispy and juicy, can be cooked in grill ovens. This works for up to 90 minutes and helps brown several types of food.

Solo Oven

A single-type oven is a basic, consistently heating oven that is mostly used for quick baking or reheating. Useful if you don't have any huge intentions for cooking.

An oven over a range

These ovens may be mounted on the wall above your stovetop and include both an oven and a range hood. To save your room, this essentially combines the microwave and the ventilation unit.

Integrated Oven

The kitchen cabinets themselves can accommodate these microwave ovens. The benefits include flexibility in the placement, a cleaner appearance for your kitchen, and counter space savings.

A stovetop oven

When installing a microwave oven, many individuals do not want to change the layout of their kitchen. Therefore, countertop ovens are a wonderful option.

How to Cook in a Microwave Oven

Maintaining moisture and ensuring an even cooking time are the two most important aspects of microwave cooking.

Microwave ovens are useful to have in the kitchen since they can cook food more quickly than a regular oven while also defrosting and reheating food.

But using a microwave to cook food is more difficult than it appears. Maintaining moisture and ensuring an even cooking time are the two most important aspects of microwave cooking.

1. **Some foods require more time to prepare than others.**

You should split the items according to how much time they require to cook. Larger, thicker foods require more time to cook than smaller foods.

The longest cooking times are often required for starchy vegetables like sweet and regular potatoes , followed by other vegetables and then meat.

2. **Increase Food Size to Shorten Cooking Time**

By dividing items into smaller amounts, you can speed up the microwave cooking process. If you cut large pieces of meat into smaller pieces, they will cook more quickly.

This method helps speed up the cooking of huge chunks of meat, other large vegetables, and potatoes.

3. **Consuming Foods with Pierced Skin**

Foods with skins have a greater capacity to retain the steam, which increases the risk of an explosion or spatter in the microwave. Use a fork or a sharp knife to make a few holes in meals like sweet and regular potatoes, hot dogs and sausages.

4. **Properly Distribute Food on a Microwave-Safe Dish**

Always cook in a dish or bowl that can be used in a microwave. The thickest portion of the food should be toward the dish's edge, and the food should be distributed equally. Food in the center cooks slower than food at the edges, therefore this aids in distributing the cooking time evenly.

Make sure to never use metal kitchen utensils and metal dishes and containers to cook in the microwave; glass and ceramic dishes are often safe to use.

5. Before cooking, cover the food.

Put the lid on the dish if it has one and allow a small opening for steam to escape if your dish has a lid. In the absence of lids, cover the dish with a wet towel or a piece of paper.

Food should be covered to guarantee consistent cooking, to keep it moist, and to avoid splatters that you will have to clean up afterward.

6. Cook in brief bursts while stirring frequently.

Set the timer and shut the microwave lid. Start by pressing the button. Cook meat at three-minute intervals, larger vegetables at two-minute intervals, and smaller vegetables at one-minute intervals. To distribute heat evenly throughout the dish, stir thoroughly between cooking cycles.

7. Before serving, let the food stand.

When your meal is finished cooking, close the microwave door and let it there to cool. This allows the meal enough time to complete cooking. Meat should stand for 10-15 minutes, while vegetables and casseroles should do so for 5-10.

What is the utilization of microwave ovens historically?

How was the microwave oven discovered? What is it? Percy LeBaron Spencer, a self-taught engineer who worked for Raytheon, was the man who accidentally created this kitchen appliance. He discovered that the chocolate bar in his pocket had melted as he was working on the vacuum tubes, also known as magnetrons, that produce microwave radiation in 1945. He began experimenting with different foods, including popcorn kernels and an egg that shook and exploded, since he was intrigued by this phenomenon. He constructed a metal enclosure to receive microwave power after realizing that the meal had been subjected to low-density microwave energy. Spencer's discovery that food would cook more quickly in this device than in a convection oven led to the patenting of this technology.

The first commercial microwave oven was tested at a Boston restaurant in 1947. Later the same year, Raytheon released the Rearrange 1161, but it took years for the public to embrace this new technology, with only 4% of people purchasing it at the time. Over time, microwave ovens gained popularity over dishwashers, shrunk in size, and became more reasonably priced.

Benefits of cooking with a Microwave

Power, time, and technique are nutrients.

The trick? determining the precise amount of time required to cook food. It's not a game of speculation.

Yes, heat does in fact decompose a few nutrients. But when using the proper technique, cooking in a microwave rather than on a stovetop maintains more of the components in veggies and fruits. A timer and the demand for perfect cooking are unmitigated ruins. It is best to undercook your food initially before cooking it for a short while longer than to overcook it. For instance, it might take our microwave 2 to 3 minutes to prepare a cup of green peas on High. If you cover the bowl with a silicon microwave-safe lid, there is typically enough ice to help steam the peas. Nutrient retention is improved by cooking peas for just two minutes, shaking the mixture halfway through, cooking for an additional minute while stirring, and then allowing the remaining peas to finish cooking. If you cook the peas on the stovetop in a tiny vessel including a ½ cup of water, you are at potential for boiling off the micronutrients. A 2009 Food Science Journal study report examined 20 home-cooked vegetables for antioxidants and found the influence of cooking methods on vegetable antioxidant activity.

The methods that produce the least waste are grilling, cooking in the microwave, and baking; those that produce the most waste are boiling, and the one that produces the most waste is frying. In other words, When it comes to cooking veggies, water is not a cook's best friend.

Convenience

More than you may imagine, a microwave can cook.

Here are some examples.

- Foods heat up and defrost more quickly in microwaves than in other ways. Dinner, lunch, and all three are included.
- Anything that can be placed within a food container that can be heated in a microwave, such as soups, mac and cheese, and popcorn, can be eaten as a snack in a matter of minutes..
- Aside from that, there are a tonne of recipes you can use to help you cook wonderful meals in a lot less time than if you were slaving over a stove..

Conserve energy

Microwave ovens use the least amount of energy of any oven or stove since they heat the water in the meal directly. The sort and calibre of cookware you employ on a cooktop will have an impact on how rapidly heat will transfer from the heat to whatever is in your cookware. The amount of cooling you need to run in the summer is not increased by microwaves, they do not keep heat, and they do not heat the entire kitchen. When you have direct control over the duration of the cooking process, you have far more control over how much electricity you consume.

Dangers of Excessive Heat

Be mindful of the equipment you use to microwave meals.

The use of microwave ovens has brought to light various issues with contemporary methods of food preparation. Even though some plastics can be used for microwave cooking, research indicates there are a few key safety considerations.

1) Avoid using Type 7 "Other" plastics.

It is recognized to have potentially negative health consequences on a child's or fetus's prostate gland and brain. The interior food cans' exteriors and consumer goods including Chemicals can leak into food from polycarbonate water bottles, food packing containers, tableware, and infant bottles..

2) Recycle it after it runs out.

Replace or recycle your microwave-safe plates if they start to look worn.

Plastics made of PVC are produced using phthalates (Type 3). When utilized for packaging, such as food packaging film, since it frequently leaks into the items. The greatest risk is seen with persistent exposure to phthalates, which are endocrine disruptor chemicals (EDCs).

Phthalates are typically present even though they are not required for the formation of PP. It was demonstrated that the greater the heat exposure to a plastic container, and utilized, the higher the phthalates it produces. Because plastic containers consistently develop malformations and avoid overheating with usage, more phthalates can contaminate food. It's time to recycle your preferred plastic food warmer if it has scars, creases, or wrinkles.

3) A Fantastic Stove Alternative

Do not misunderstand us; we love using the stove to cook excellent meals for our household. Some delicacies are simply impossible to replicate in a microwave! We want to demonstrate to you that heating up a lot of the meals we frequently eat in your microwave is quite okay. Along with being practical, frequently using a microwave for cooking could help you spend less energy each month..

Foods Never to Be Put in a Microwave Oven

While you can microwave a variety of foods to enjoy them hot and crispy, you should avoid doing so with others.

These consist of:

- Avoid attempting to hard boil an egg in a microwave because it will explode due to the build-up of steam inside the shell.
- Avoid breathing in the fumes from chili peppers because the spice in them vaporizes.
- Try to avoid boiling water because sometimes the water only serves to warm the mug. The water may overheat when the tea is added and swirled, perhaps blowing the mug away.
- Breast milk should be microwaved cautiously since, if taken out of the freezer, it may become heated in some parts and remain cold in others. In this instance, microwave cooking is dangerous.
- Even though processed foods are inherently unhealthy, microwaving them causes the development of cholesterol oxidation products, which have previously been linked to heart disease.
- Avoid using leafy greens in the microwave since some of them might catch fire and potentially burn both your food and the equipment. Extreme caution is advised!
- Olive oil, peanut oil, avocado oil, and other types of oils should not be heated because they are fats rather than liquids. They can be heated, although it might not be successful.
- Fruits shouldn't be roasted because doing so makes the inside of them extremely hot, which might burn your palate.
- Because rice contains specific bacteria that can only be eliminated by boiling it on the stove, it is not a good idea to cook rice in the microwave.
- Fruit that has been frozen shouldn't be heated; instead, it should be defrosted to prevent the excellent qualities from becoming carcinogenic.

Guidelines to Bear in Mind Whenever Using a Microwave

Care should be used when using ovens. Do you notice anything about your microwave oven that might be a cause for concern? Make sure to have a corporate representative inspect it.

Following are some pointers for utilizing ng a microwave oven:

1. Avoid using plastic or metal in the oven.
2. For the food to heat properly, try to distribute it evenly.
3. Avoid cooking foods that call for a lot of water.
4. Regularly combine and stir.
5. To stop spills, cover the bowl or mug.
6. To make things like potatoes and hotdogs warm on the inside, prick them with a fork.
7. The faster the meal cooks, the smaller the bits are.
8. When thawing food, use the defrost setting.

FAQs

1. Are baby bottles safe to microwave?

Being a mother can be challenging because there are so many decisions that must be taken for the baby's welfare. New mothers frequently ask this query when they are uncertain whether to microwave the baby bottle. Although it is not advisable, baby bottles can be microwaved without endangering the child. The heating process destroys the immune qualities of breast milk. However, cow's milk or infant formula can be cooked without any problems.

2. What Happens When You Stand Next to a Running Microwave Oven?

The technology in microwave ovens is advanced enough to prevent harmful radio radiation from invading your body. The door has tiny squares or circles that serve as a shield since they have a shorter wavelength than a microwave. Generally speaking, if you stand close to a microwave, nothing will happen. On the other hand, standing close to one for extended periods might not be healthy either.

3. Can Food Be Microwaved in a Plastic Container?

Considering all the meal delivery applications at your fingertips, ordering food online has grown increasingly popular in recent years. The majority of eateries sell their meals in microwave-safe containers. Any plastic cannot be used in a microwave since it will probably melt. You must utilize unique microwave-safe dishes, mugs, and containers that can endure the heat without melting into your food and ruining your meal.

4. Is Using a Microwave Oven Safe While Pregnant?

According to certain studies, electromagnetic waves from microwave ovens may not be the greatest for women who are pregnant and their unborn children. The use of a microwave has various drawbacks. Because microwaves can harm embryos and cause a miscarriage, it is even more important to avoid using one that is old or defective. It is always preferable to be safe than sorry even though no research conclusively demonstrates its negative effects.

Most of the technology that is currently available was created by humans. One of the simple technical miracles that we take for granted is the ability to instantly reheat food. For several reasons, microwave ovens have altered the playing field. Ovens are very useful and safe if used correctly per the microwave cooking recommendations, despite the fact that some people may argue against their use due to their negative impact on our health. Take care, savor a warm supper, and the next time, stop to appreciate the microwave.

Breakfast Recipes

Cheesy Omelette

Serve : 1 |Time : 05 minutes

Cal|484 Fat| 40.7 g Protein| 27.4 g Fiber| 0.3 g Cholesterol | 463 mg

Ingredients

- ❖ 15 ml olive oil
- ❖ 15 g chopped green onion, optional
- ❖ 5 g dried basil
- ❖ 15 ml almond milk
- ❖ 2 large eggs
- ❖ Pinch of kosher salt
- ❖ Pinch of freshly ground black pepper
- ❖ 64 g grated Parmesan cheese

Directions

1. The oil, green onion and basil should all be combined in a large mug. Microwave for 15 seconds, or until the oil heated. As you whisk until foamy, add the milk and eggs. Add the cheese, pepper, and salt after that. The egg should be hard after another minute in the microwave. Serve right away.

Blackberry Muffin

Serve: 1 |Time: 02 minutes

Cal|188 Fat| 9.5 g Protein| 9.9 g Fiber| 5.1 g Cholesterol | 186 mg

Ingredients

* 15 g all-purpose flour
* 15 g Wheat flour.
* 15 g quinoa flour
* 30 ml honey
* 3 g baking powder

* Pinch nutmeg
* 1 large egg
* 15 ml oil
* 15 ml almond milk
* 15- 30 g frozen blackberries

Directions

1. The flours, nutmeg, and baking powder should all be thoroughly mixed together in a small basin.
2. Add your egg, honey, oil and almond milk, then stir everything up thoroughly. Make sure there are a few blueberries left on top before folding in the blueberries.
3. Depending on your microwave, heat for 50 seconds (or up to 2 minutes), then remove. Enjoy right away.

Egg Scramble

Serve: 1 |Time: 02 minutes

Cal|219 Fat| 15.6 g Protein| 16.7 g Fiber| 0.3 g Cholesterol | 204 mg

Ingredients

- ❖ 1 egg
- ❖ 30 g chopped mushrooms
- ❖ 1 thin slice cooked bacon
- ❖ 30 g shredded Swiss cheese

Directions

1. APPLY cooking spray to a 12-ounce coffee cup that is microwave-safe. Add the egg, water, ham, mushrooms, and beat until well combined. 30 seconds on HIGH in the microwave; stir. MICROWAVE egg for a further 30 to 45 seconds, or until almost set.
2. SEASON, if preferred, with salt and pepper. Put cheese on top. SERVE right away.

French Toast Mug

Serve: 1 |Time: 02 minutes

Cal|274 Fat| 6.7 g Protein| 9.6 g Fiber| 1.2 g Cholesterol | 169 mg

Ingredients

- ❖ 1 piece buttered
- ❖ 30 ml almond milk
- ❖ 1 egg
- ❖ 15 ml honey
- ❖ 5 g ground cinnamon

- ❖ pinch of salt
- ❖ 15 g chocolate chips

Directions

1. Combine the egg, milk, honey, cinnamon, and salt during a microwave-safe mug until well-combined.
2. Slice your bread into square bits of varying sizes after removing the crusts off the edges .
3. Place the bread within the mug and firmly press it down so that it is immersed in the liquid and absorbs the egg mixture.
4. Add the chocolate chunks and provides the mixture a quick toss to combine them.
5. Optional cinnamon sugar should be sprinkled on top.
6. to stop the food from exploding in your microwave, microwave it for two minutes total, pausing every 30 seconds to count to 10 before continuing.
7. Allow to chill for a few seconds.
8. On top, sprinkling granulated sugar
9. Enjoy!

Blackberry Banana Microwave Baked Oats

Serve: 1 |Time: 10 minutes

Cal|369 Fat| 11 g Protein| 13.4 g Fiber| 8.9 g Cholesterol | 164 mg

Ingredients

- ❖ 64 g old-fashioned rolled oats
- ❖ 15 g ground chia seed
- ❖ 1 egg
- ❖ 64 ml coconut milk
- ❖ 1/3 banana, mashed
- ❖ 1 g nutmeg

- ❖ 8 g honey
- ❖ 67 g fresh blackberries

Directions

1. Cooking spray a medium to large microwave-safe mug or small dish, then add all the ingredients—aside from the blueberries—and mix well. Add blackberries next and mix.
2. 2-3 minutes on high in the microwave. (I checked my mug after two minutes and gave it one more minute to cook.)
3. If preferred, stir in additional milk, yoghurt, or nut butter.

Cinnamon Roll

Serve: 1 |Time: 10 minutes

Cal|465 Fat| 34.5 g Protein| 4.2 g Fiber| 8 g Cholesterol | 0 mg

Ingredients

- 30 g almond flour
- 4 g cinnamon
- Pinch of sea salt
- Pinch of nutmeg
- 2 g baking powder
- 1 egg

- 30 ml coconut milk
- 20 ml honey
- 15 ml coconut oil
- 2 g vanilla extract

Directions

1. In a mug, combine all the ingredients for a cinnamon roll, adding the baking powder last.
2. 2 minutes on high in the microwave.
3. The icing ingredients should be combined in a small bowl in the meanwhile.
4. Over the steaming cinnamon bun, drizzle frosting.
5. Go ahead!

Strawberry Banana Baked Oatmeal in a Mug

Serve: 1 |Time: 10 minutes

Cal|319 Fat| 8.6 g Protein| 12.9 g Fiber| 6.3 g Cholesterol | 167 mg

Ingredients

- ❖ 64 g old-fashioned oats
- ❖ 4 g coconut sugar
- ❖ 2 g baking powder
- ❖ Dash of salt
- ❖ ½ medium banana, mashed
- ❖ 1 egg

- ❖ 45 ml almond milk
- ❖ 1.45 g vanilla extract
- ❖ 3 medium strawberries, diced

Directions

1. Apply cooking spray to a big, microwave-safe mug or a small bowl. To the mug, add salt, baking soda, coconut sugar, and oats. To blend, stir.
2. Oats are combined with banana, egg, almond milk, and vanilla essence. Mix in by stirring. Strawberries should be added gently.
3. 3 to 3 1/2 minutes on medium power, or until the centre is mostly set, in the microwave. Allow the microwave to stand for one minute.
4. Serve right away.

Veggie Mug Omelette

Serve: 1 | Time: 10 minutes

Cal| 294 Fat| 15.3 g Protein| 19.9 g Fiber| 3.8 g Cholesterol | 387 mg

Ingredients

- ❖ 2 large eggs
- ❖ 30 ml soy milk
- ❖ 30 g shredded goat cheese
- ❖ 30 g finely diced red pepper
- ❖ 30 g finely diced green pepper

- ❖ 30 g roughly chopped fresh kale
- ❖ Salt and pepper, to taste

Directions

1. Prepare: Grease a sizable coffee mug lightly.
2. Combination: Add the milk and eggs to the mug and stir to blend. Add cheese, peppers, and spinach after mixing.
3. Cooking Instructions: Microwave the egg on high for 1 to 2 minutes, stirring after 30 seconds.
4. Serve hot and season with salt and pepper.

Egg Muffin

Serve: 1 |Time: 10 minutes

Cal| 313 Fat| 15.5 g Protein| 10.7 g Fiber| 1.2 g Cholesterol | 123 mg

Ingredients

- ❖ 75 g coconut flour
- ❖ 1.5 g baking powder
- ❖ Pinch of baking soda
- ❖ Pinch of salt
- ❖ 30 ml almond milk
- ❖ 10 ml vegetable oil

- ❖ 15 g grated cheddar cheese
- ❖ 15 g green onion chopped
- ❖ 2 small egg

Directions

1. With a fork, combine the flour, baking soda, baking powder, and salt in a sizable microwave-safe mug.
2. As soon as everything is blended, add the milk, oil, egg, cheese, and scallions.
3. With the aid of a spoon, create a well in the middle of the batter and add the egg.
4. Over the egg, spoon the remaining batter from the edges. Although a little challenging, you'll manage.
5. Cook for 50–1–10 seconds in the microwave after placing the food there. Its top will feel solid to the touch when it is fully cooked, letting you know. (Your timing may vary; cooking time is based on my 1200W microwave.) To avoid spilling or overcooking, always keep a close check on your mug while it's being heated in the microwave.
6. Savour the warmth

Peach oatmeal

Serve: 1 |Time: 10 minutes

Cal| 179 Fat| 2.7 g Protein| 5.4 g Fiber| 4.6 g Cholesterol | 0 mg

Ingredients

- 30 g old fashioned oats
- 64 ml water
- 30 g sliced peaches in juice,
- Pinch of cinnamon
- Pinch of vanilla extract

- 3 g coconut sugar (optional)

Directions

1. Slice up the peaches into small pieces.
2. Oats, water, and peaches with juice are added to a bowl.
3. Cook food at 1-minute intervals using a 500-watt microwave after cooking it for 2 minutes, stirring, and another 2 minutes. In a 1200-watt microwave, heat the food for 30 seconds, stir, and then cook it for an additional 30 seconds at 30-second intervals.
4. Add cinnamon, butterscotch extract, and sweetener after cooking.

Poaching Eggs

Serve: 1 |Time: 10 minutes

Cal| 72 Fat| 5 g Protein| 6.3 g Fiber| 0 g Cholesterol | 186 mg

Ingredients

- ❖ 1large egg
- ❖ Pinch of lemon juice
- ❖ 80 ml water
- ❖ salt and pepper

Directions

1. A 6-ounce custard cup should now include both water and lemon juice.
2. Egg yolk should be poked with a toothpick before dish is loosely covered with plastic wrap.
3. Cook in the microwave for one minute, or until the desired doneness.
4. Depending on your microwave's power and personal preferences, you might need to experiment with cooking times.
5. With a slotted spoon, quickly take the egg from the hot water since it will continue to cook.
6. Add salt and pepper to taste when serving.

Egg Frittata

Serve: 1 | Time: 10 minutes

Cal| 72 Fat| 5 g Protein| 6.3 g Fiber| 0 g Cholesterol | 186 mg

Ingredients

- ❖ 2 eggs
- ❖ 60 ml coconut milk
- ❖ 64 g fresh kale leaves
- ❖ 1 roma tomato
- ❖ 1 -2 slice bacon
- ❖ 45 g shredded goat cheese

- ❖ Cooking spray
- ❖ salt and pepper

Directions

1. Apply cooking spray to a cereal-sized bowl that's safe for the microwave.
2. After washing, drying, and removing the stems, the spinach should be torn into bite-sized pieces. (I'd say around half a cup; I generally just take a touch fistful.) Toss into bowl's base.
3. Slice or dice the tomato, then throw it inches away. The bacon is that the same. Then, sprinkle cheese on top.
4. Pour the milk and two eggs over the mess at the underside of the bowl after lightly beating them with a fork in a separate cup.
5. 3 minutes on high within the microwave. A nasty crust of crispy egg will emerge if you overcook the food. It gets fluffier the faster you consume it. it'll be chilly and roughly half the size it was when it came out of the microwave after 15 minutes. i do not suggest allowing it to sit for so long.

Tasty Oatmeal

Serve: 1 |Time: 10 minutes

Cal| 72 Fat| 5 g Protein| 6.3 g Fiber| 0 g Cholesterol | 186 mg

Ingredients

- ❖ 240 ml water
- ❖ 64 g rolled oats
- ❖ 1 dash salt
- ❖ 30 g coconut sugar

- ❖ 30 g chopped pecans
- ❖ 30 g dried cherries

Directions

1. In a dish or pot that can be used in the microwave, combine the ingredients. Stir after two minutes and twenty seconds in the microwave. If "watery," nuke for ten to fifteen seconds.

Granola

Serve: 8 |Time: 10 minutes

Cal| 254 Fat| 10.8 g Protein| 5.6 g Fiber| 3.5 g Cholesterol | 16 mg

Ingredients

- ❖ 495 g oats
- ❖ 110 g chopped nuts,
- ❖ 110 ml honey
- ❖ 55 g butter (cut into pieces)
- ❖ 7 g cinnamon

- ❖ 55 g wheat germ
- ❖ 110 g dried fruit, of your choice

Directions

1. In a bowl that can go in the microwave, combine all the ingredients minus the dried fruit.
2. Cook for two minutes on high.
3. Cook for 2 minutes longer while stirring.
4. After removing from the microwave, stir in the dried fruit.
5. Spread out to cool on a big cookie sheet.
6. In an airtight container, store.

Rice Bran-Banana

Serve: 1 |Time: 10 minutes

Cal| 254 Fat| 10.8 g Protein| 5.6 g Fiber| 3.5 g Cholesterol | 16 mg

Ingredients

- ❖ 1⁄2 banana, chopped
- ❖ 70 g rice bran
- ❖ 1dash salt
- ❖ 180 ml water

- ❖ 4 g maple syrup

Directions

1. Combine the diced banana, rice bran, salt, water, and sugar in a microwave-safe bowl
2. Microwave for three minutes on high, whisking every minute.
3. If using, maple syrup should be added after cooking.
4. If you'd like, milk can be provided.

Sour Cream Poached Eggs

Serve: 1 |Time: 10 minutes

Cal| 377 Fat| 32.8 g Protein| 15 g Fiber| 0.5 g Cholesterol | 376 mg

Ingredients

- ❖ 115-g sour cream
- ❖ 2 eggs
- ❖ 1 scallion, chopped
- ❖ 1dash paprika

Directions

1. In a microwave-safe container, place the sour cream.
2. Add the green onion, chopped.
3. In the sour cream, make a well, then add the two eggs.
4. When the whites are done, cover and microwave at 60% power for 2 1/2 to 3 1/2 minutes.
5. Toast is served with paprika sprinkled on top.

Apricot & Berry Mug Pancake

Serve: 1 |Time: 10 minutes

Cal| 177 Fat| 4.5 g Protein| 3.6 g Fiber| 2.5 g Cholesterol | 8 mg

Ingredients

- ❖ 35 g complete pancake mix
- ❖ Approximately 60 ml of water
- ❖ 2 apricots, pits removed and cut in half.
- ❖ 4-6 fresh berries
- ❖ 35 g pecan halves
- ❖ Honey for serving

Directions

1. 1/4 of a big mug should be filled with the pancake batter (the kind that only requires water).
2. Add water to the mug until it is halfway filled. Blend the mixture and water thoroughly.
3. Combine the batter with half of the berries, apricots, and pecans.
4. Add the remaining fruit and nuts on top after 2 minutes on high in the microwave.
5. Continue to microwave for another 30 to 60 seconds, or until set. Add honey to the dish.

Cinnamon chia Seed Muffin

Serve: 2 |Time: 05 minutes

Cal| 326 Fat| 28.5 g Protein| 6.7 g Fiber| 8.9 g Cholesterol | 12.8 mg

Ingredients

- ❖ 30 g almond Flour
- ❖ 15 g chia seed meal
- ❖ 1.5 g Baking powder
- ❖ 1 pinch Sea salt
- ❖ 1 large Egg
- ❖ 45 ml oil

- ❖ 30 g coconut sugar
- ❖ 10 g Cinnamon

Directions

1. Sea salt, gluten-free baking powder, chia seed meal, and almond flour should all be combined in a cup. Add 15 g coconut sugar, or half of it, if you're preparing one serving.
2. Add the oil and egg. As you stir, make sure there are no dry ingredients remaining at the bottom. Stir thoroughly until smooth. Allow to thicken for a minute.
3. Optional step: Depending on your almond flour, you can thin out the batter with water or your preferred milk if it is too stiff. If you choose to do this, add the liquid by teaspoonful until the mixture is thin enough. The amount depends on the brand of coconut flour you're using; it should be simple to stir but not liquid.
4. Combine the remaining coconut sugar and cinnamon in a small bowl. On top of the batter, put the cinnamon mixture into the centre of the mug. Use a spoon to gently swirl the mixture a couple of times. With the back of a spoon, level the top.
5. until set, microwave on high for 1 to 2 minutes. (If you'd rather use the oven, bake in an oven-safe ramekin for 10–20 minutes, depending on the form of your ramekin, at 350 degrees F [177 degrees C]).

Pumpkin Spice Muffin

Serve: 1 |Time: 10 minutes

Cal| 579 Fat| 8.5 g Protein| 26.1 g Fiber| 10.5 g Cholesterol | 10 mg

Ingredients

- ❖ 1 large whole egg
- ❖ 75 g Pumpkin Puree Organic
- ❖ 45 g Ground chia seed Meal
- ❖ 4 g maple syrup
- ❖ 4 g oil
- ❖ 2 g Spices, pumpkin pie spice

Directions

1. In a sizable coffee mug that is microwave-safe, crack an egg. Beat lightly with a fork.
2. Combine the flaxseed meal, pumpkin pie spice, coconut oil, honey, and pumpkin puree.
3. Two minutes on high in the microwave; keep an eye out to make sure the muffin doesn't rise above the rim of the mug.
4. Either eat the muffin directly from the cup or turn it over onto a small plate and top it with more cinnamon.

Blueberry and Oatmeal Muffin

Serve: 1 |Time: 10 minutes

Cal| 261 Fat| 7.2 g Protein| 11.2 g Fiber| 5 g Cholesterol | 164 mg

Ingredients

- ❖ 40 g dry oatmeal
- ❖ 120 ml water
- ❖ 1 Egg
- ❖ 4 g maple syrup
- ❖ 4 g Baking Powder
- ❖ 4 g chia seeds
- ❖ 30 g Fresh Blueberries

Directions

1. In a LARGE coffee mug, combine the oatmeal, honey, and water and stir until all the oats are moist.
2. Microwave oatmeal for two minutes on HIGH or until steaming hot.
   Stir the oatmeal and allow it to cool for a minute.
3. Add baking soda, chia seeds, and fresh blueberries to the mixture.
4. Add 1 raw egg and thoroughly combine.
5. Return to the microwave and cook for about a minute on HIGH. (Keep an eye on it; it might overflow!)
6. Return the muffin to the microwave for another 20 seconds if it doesn't appear firm.
7. When ready, place the mug on a dish upside down. For decoration, you might also slice some fresh strawberries.

Lunch Recipes

Ranch Chicken Tacos

Serve: 4 |Time: 25 minutes

Cal| 504 Fat| 27 g Protein| 29.5 g Fiber| 8 g Cholesterol | 86 mg

Ingredients

- ❖ 64 g ranch dressing
- ❖ 64 g reduced-fat sour cream
- ❖ 28 g taco seasoning mix, divided
- ❖ 15 g mild chunky salsa
- ❖ 280 g shredded rotisserie chicken
- ❖ 8 (6 inch) corn tortillas
- ❖ shredded lettuce
- ❖ 1 tomato, chopped
- ❖ 4 green onions, sliced
- ❖ 110 g can have sliced black olives
- ❖ 140 g shredded Colby-Monterey Jack cheese

Directions

1. In a small bowl, mix salsa, ranch dressing, sour cream, and 1 teaspoon taco seasoning. With a cover on, chill until serving.
2. Chicken is mixed with the remaining taco seasoning. Wrap plastic wrap or wax paper loosely around the bowl. Cook the chicken in the microwave for 2 to 3 minutes, or until well heated.
3. To soften tortillas, heat them in a skillet for about a minute on each side. A dollop of the ranch dressing mixture should be added to the tortilla along with a scoop of chicken, lettuce, tomato, green onion, olives, and cheese.

Prawns Biryani

Serve: 2 |Time: 25 minutes

Cal| 504 Fat| 27 g Protein| 29.5 g Fiber| 8 g Cholesterol | 86 mg

Ingredients

- 170 g cups uncooked rice
- 255 g prawns
- 15 g ginger garlic paste
- 4 g Garam masala
- 4 g ground black pepper
- 4 whole cloves
- 4 whole cardamom seeds
- 2 cinnamon sticks
- salt to taste
- 110 g coconut yogurt
- 54 ml vegetable oil
- 240 ml water

Directions

1. Place the rice and sufficient water to soak it in a small bowl. After soaking the rice for two hours, drain it.
2. 2. In a microwave-safe bowl, combine the prawns, cinnamon sticks, Garam masala, whole cloves, entire cardamom seeds, cinnamon sticks, salt, coconut yoghurt, crushed black pepper, ginger-garlic paste and oil. swirl to thoroughly combine. Cook the shrimp in the microwave for about 10 minutes on High, or until the interior is opaque and the outsides are a vibrant pink colour. Remove the prawns from the curry and set them aside.
3. The rice, water, and curry should be completely combined. Rice should be microwaved on High for around 10 minutes. After blending, add the shrimp and reheat on high for 5 minutes, or until thoroughly heated. Remove the cinnamon stick, cloves, and cardamom seeds before serving.

Risotto

Serve: 4 |Time: 25 minutes

Cal| 406 Fat|14.5 g Protein| 12.7 g Fiber| 2.1 g Cholesterol | 39 mg

Ingredients

- ❖ 45 g butter
- ❖ 1 clove garlic, minced
- ❖ 1 onion, chopped
- ❖ 355 ml vegetable broth
- ❖ 210 g uncooked Arborio rice
- ❖ 175 ml white wine
- ❖ 85 g grated Parmesan cheese

Directions

1. Combine butter, garlic, and onion in a 3-quart casserole dish that can be used in the microwave. Cook the meal in the microwave for three minutes on high.
2. Fill a bowl that can be microwaved with veggie broth. Heat the broth in the microwave until it is hot but not boiling (approximately 2 minutes).
3. Rice and stock are added to the onion, butter, and garlic mixture in the casserole dish. Cook the dish for 6 minutes on high with a tight cover.
4. Rice and wine are combined. Cook for a further ten minutes on high. Most of the liquid ought should evaporate. Serve the rice after incorporating the cheese.

Romano Chicken

Serve: 6 |Time: 20 minutes

Cal| 406 Fat|14.5 g Protein| 12.7 g Fiber| 2.1 g Cholesterol | 39 mg

Ingredients

- 4 skinless, boneless chicken breast halves - pounded to 1/4-inch thickness
- 115 g Swiss cheese, sliced
- 115 g ham, sliced thin
- 30 g grated Parmesan cheese
- 6 g paprika
- 2 g garlic salt
- 2 g dried tarragon
- 2 g dried basil leaves
- 15 g butter, melted
- 70 g dry bread crumbs

Directions

1. On a pan, arrange the chicken breasts. Roll up the Swiss cheese and ham pieces with the aid of toothpicks if necessary. Combine the bread crumbs, Parmesan cheese, paprika, garlic salt, tarragon, and basil in a small bowl. Combine, then coat rollups by dipping them in the mixture.
2. Drizzle the chicken with melted butter and microwave on High for 4 minutes, or until the chicken is well cooked and the juices flow clear.

Baked Potato

Serve: 1 |Time: 10 minutes

Cal| 474 Fat|19.1 g Protein| 11.9 g Fiber| 6.9g Cholesterol | 51 mg

Ingredients

- ❖ 1 large russet potato
- ❖ as desired, add salt and black pepper
- ❖ 15 g butter
- ❖ 30 g shredded Cheddar cheese
- ❖ 15 g sour cream

Directions

1. Potato should be scrubbed and forked. Put on a plate that can be used in a microwave.
2. 5 minutes at maximum power in the microwave. Microwave potato for an additional five minutes or until soft on the other side.
3. Cut the microwaved potato in half lengthwise after removing it. Add salt and pepper, then use a fork to slightly mash up the interior.
4. Cheese and butter should be added. For about another minute, microwave until melted.
5. Serve after adding sour cream on top.

Spanish Rice

Serve: 4 |Time: 40 minutes

Cal| 474 Fat|19.1 g Protein| 11.9 g Fiber| 6.9g Cholesterol | 51 mg

Ingredients

- 210 g white rice
- ½ onion, chopped
- 540 g whole peeled tomatoes
- 240 ml water
- 85 g diced green bell pepper
-

- 85 ml ketchup
- 4 g salt
- 2 g chili powder
- 1 dash ground black pepper

Directions

1. In the baking dish, combine the rice and onion. Microwave for four minutes, or until just soft. Add the chopped cooked bacon, tomatoes, ketchup, water, green pepper, salt, and pepper.
2. For 10 minutes, microwave covered. Cooking mixture for a further 8 minutes or more, stirring occasionally, until rice is cooked and flavours are well-balanced. Before serving, allow to cool briefly.

Chicken Parmesan

Serve: 4 |Time: 50 minutes

Cal| 527 Fat|17.4 g Protein| 42.1 g Fiber| 7.3g Cholesterol | 164 mg

Ingredients

- ❖ 4 skinless, boneless chicken breasts
- ❖ 240 g Italian-seasoned bread crumbs
- ❖ 240 g grated Parmesan cheese
- ❖ 15 g smoked paprika
- ❖ 4 g dried parsley flakes

- ❖ 2 eggs
- ❖ olive oil cooking spray
- ❖ 800 g jar chunky marinara sauce
- ❖ 480 g shredded mozzarella cheese
- ❖ 8 g crushed oregano

Directions

1. On a sturdy, flat surface, sandwich chicken breasts between two sheets of heavy plastic. Use a meat mallet's smooth side to firmly pound the meat to a thickness of 1/2 inch.
2. Shake the ingredients for bread crumbs, Parmesan cheese, paprika, and parsley flakes in a sizable plastic bag that can be sealed.
3. In a small basin, beat eggs. Chicken breasts are dredged in bread crumbs after being dipped in beaten eggs. Each chicken breast is dipped and coated once more.
4. Cooking spray should be used to coat a microwave-safe dish big enough to accommodate chicken breasts in a single layer. In the dish, arrange the breaded chicken breasts. Apply cooking spray to the chicken breasts' tops.
5. 6 minutes of cooking at 50% power in the microwave. Chicken breasts should be covered in marinara sauce. For 12 minutes, cook with the cover on at full power. Over the sauce, top with mozzarella cheese and oregano. Dish should be covered and let out for 10 minutes or so for the mozzarella cheese to melt.

Couscous Salad with Tomato and Basil

Serve: 6 |Time: 25 minutes

Cal| 81 Fat|3.9 g Protein| 2.8 g Fiber| 1.2g Cholesterol | 6 mg

Ingredients

- 30ml olive oil
- 2 cloves garlic, minced
- 410 ml fat-free, reduced-sodium chicken broth
- 270 g couscous
- 360 g chopped tomato

- 70 g thinly sliced fresh basil
- 30 ml balsamic vinegar
- 2 g salt
- 1 g ground black pepper
- 85 g crumbled feta cheese

Directions

1. In a sizable microwave-safe bowl, combine 15 ml olive oil and the garlic. Microwave on high for about 45 seconds, or until aromatic. For about 4 minutes, add chicken broth and cook on high until simmering. As you stir, add the couscous. Cover and leave in place for 5 minutes or until liquid is absorbed. Make couscous fluffy with a fork.
2. Combine the couscous with the tomato, basil, vinegar, salt, and black pepper. Drizzle the dish with the remaining 15 ml of olive oil and top with the feta cheese.

Meat Loaf

Serve: 6 |Time: 45 minutes

Cal| 322 Fat|11.5 g Protein| 42.8 g Fiber| 1.1g Cholesterol | 169 mg

Ingredients

- ❖ 225 g tomato sauce
- ❖ 85 g brown sugar
- ❖ 4 g prepared mustard
- ❖ 2 eggs, lightly beaten
- ❖ 1 onion, minced
- ❖ 85 g minced green bell pepper

- ❖ 1 g garlic powder
- ❖ 170 g cracker crumbs
- ❖ 1 teaspoon salt
- ❖ 1 g ground black pepper
- ❖ 900 g extra lean ground beef

Directions

1. Brown sugar, mustard, and tomato sauce should be combined in a small bowl; stir until the brown sugar is dissolved.
2. The eggs, minced onion and green pepper, garlic powder, cracker crumbs, salt, and black pepper should all be incorporated in a large bowl before adding the ground beef and half of the tomato sauce mixture. Stir until the meat loaf is well combined. Put the beef mixture in a 2-quart baking dish that can be used in the microwave. Over the meat loaf, spread the remaining tomato sauce mixture.
3. Cook in a microwave oven on High for 10 to 15 minutes, depending on the power of the appliance, or until the meat is set, the juices run clear, and the interior is no longer pink. The internal temperature of the loaf should register 165 degrees Fahrenheit on an instant-read meat thermometer (75 degrees C). As soon as the bread is through cooking, drain any remaining grease from the pan. Let the meal stand 10 to 15 minutes before serving, uncovered.

Easy Stuffed Peppers

Serve: 4|Time: 30 minutes

Cal| 134 Fat|1.7 g Protein| 5.2 g Fiber| 4g Cholesterol | 26.1 mg

Ingredients

- ❖ 2 green bell peppers, halved and seeded
- ❖ 220 g tomatoes, with liquid
- ❖ 65 g white rice
- ❖ 30 ml hot water
- ❖ 2 scallion , thinly sliced

- ❖ 100 g corn kernels, thawed and drained
- ❖ 180 g black beans, drained and rinsed
- ❖ 1 g red pepper flakes
- ❖ 100 g shredded goat cheese
- ❖ 15 g grated Parmesan cheese

Directions

1. Place pepper halves in a glass baking dish that is 9 inches square. Dish with plastic wrap on it. Make a few vent holes in the plastic wrap, then microwave the food for 4 minutes, or until it is soft.
2. Combine rice, water, and tomato juice in a medium bowl. Cook rice in the microwave for 4 minutes, or until done. Cover with plastic.
3. The tomato mixture should be mixed with green onions, corn, kidney beans, and red pepper flakes. 3 minutes, or until thoroughly heated, in the microwave.
4. Pepper halves should be uniformly topped with a hot tomato mixture before being wrapped in plastic. To release steam, poke a few holes in the plastic. Then, microwave for 4 minutes. Before serving, take off the plastic wrap, top with mozzarella and parmesan cheese, and let stand for 1 to 2 minutes.

BBQ Chicken Chopped Salad

Serve: 6|Time: 20 minutes

Cal| 732 Fat|13.7 g Protein| 36 g Fiber| 26.1g Cholesterol | 134 mg

Ingredients

- ❖ 1 head romaine lettuce, chopped
- ❖ 425 g black beans, rinsed and drained
- ❖ 425 g can sweet corn, drained
- ❖ 1 red bell pepper, chopped
- ❖ 130 g peeled, shredded jicama
- ❖ 130 g shredded carrots
- ❖ 4 scallions, thinly sliced
- ❖ 85 g chopped fresh basil
- ❖ 85 g chopped fresh cilantro
- ❖ 3 limes, divided
- ❖ 170 g package cooked chicken breast strips
- ❖ 30 g barbeque sauce
- ❖ 1 avocado - peeled, pitted, and cubed

Directions

1. In a sizable bowl, combine lettuce, black beans, corn, red bell pepper, jicama, carrots, onions, basil, and cilantro. Juice two limes, then drizzle the juice over the salad and gently toss.
2. Combine the chicken and barbecue sauce in a microwave-safe bowl and cook for about 45 seconds, or until the chicken is well heated.
3. Place the leftover lime juice over the salad and top with the chicken, avocado, and other ingredients.

Tuna, Avocado and Bacon Sandwich

Serve: 2|Time: 10 minutes

Cal| 798 Fat|46.4 g Protein| 49.9 g Fiber| 8.5g Cholesterol | 93mg

Ingredients

- ❖ 4 slices bacon
- ❖ 140 g solid white tuna packed in water
- ❖ 2 g Wasabi
- ❖ 2 g prepared horseradish
- ❖ 15 g sweet pickle relish
- ❖ 15 g minced onion

- ❖ 1 g paprika
- ❖ black pepper to taste
- ❖ 2 buns, split
- ❖ 1 boiled egg
- ❖ 1 tomato, sliced
- ❖ 2 slices provolone cheese
- ❖ 2 lettuce leaves

Directions

1. On a tray covered with paper towels, microwave the bacon for about 4 minutes, or until it is crispy.
2. In the meantime, tuna, Wasabi, horseradish, relish, and onion are combined. Paprika and pepper can be added for flavours. The buns should each receive a portion of this mixture. Each sandwich should contain 2 slices of bacon, 1 lettuce leaf, 1 slice of provolone cheese, 1/2 a boiled egg, ¼ a tomato, and 1 slice of lettuce.

Simple Broccoli and Cheese

Serve: 4|Time: 15 minutes

Cal| 183 Fat|13.3 g Protein| 6.1 g Fiber| 5g Cholesterol | 38mg

Ingredients

- ❖ 285 g package frozen broccoli florets, thawed
- ❖ 45 g butter, melted, or to taste
- ❖ salt and pepper to taste
- ❖ 110 g shredded Cheddar cheese

Directions

1. In a steamer with 1 inch of boiling water, add broccoli and close the lid. Cook for 2 to 6 minutes or until the food is soft yet firm. Transfer to a casserole dish that may be microwaved after draining.
2. Pour melted butter over broccoli and season with salt and pepper. Cheese should melt in the microwave on high for about a minute after being sprinkled on top.

Acorn Squash

Serve: 4|Time: 20 minutes

Cal| 136 Fat|4 g Protein| 1.9 g Fiber| 3.4g Cholesterol | 10mg

Ingredients

- ❖ 900 g acorn squash, halved and seeded
- ❖ 16 g salted butter, melted
- ❖ 16 g coconut sugar
- ❖ as desired, add salt and black pepper

Directions

1. The squash halves should be forked all over inside before being brushed with butter and dusted with coconut sugar. Put the cut sides of the squash halves up in a sizable microwave-safe dish.
2. For roughly 10 minutes on high power, until the flesh is readily pierced with a fork. Add salt and pepper to taste.

Easy Grilled Potatoes

Serve: 4|Time: 30 minutes

Cal| 187 Fat|7.2 g Protein| 3.1 g Fiber| 4.4g Cholesterol | 0mg

Ingredients

- ❖ 2 large russet potatoes, scrubbed
- ❖ 30 ml olive oil
- ❖ as desired, add salt and black pepper

Directions

1. Take a fork and prick each potato. Put the potatoes in the microwave and cook for about 5 minutes on high power. Potatoes should be checked halfway through and turned over to ensure even cooking. Cook potatoes for a further 2 minutes on high power after cutting them in half lengthwise.
2. Grill at a medium temperature.
3. Olive oil should be brushed over the potato tops before adding salt and pepper to taste.
4. Cook for 15 to 20 minutes on a preheated grill, flipping once.

Cilantro Tomato Corn Salad

Serve: 4|Time: 20 minutes

Cal| 109 Fat|11.6 g Protein| 0.4 g Fiber| 0.3g Cholesterol | 31mg

Ingredients

- 3 ears fresh corn in husks
- 55 g butter, melted
- 2 tomatoes, chopped
- 1 jalapeno pepper,
- 1 small red onion, finely chopped
- 2 cloves garlic, minced
- ½ bunch fresh cilantro, chopped

- as desired, salt and black pepper
- 1 pinch salt-free lemon-herb seasoning

Directions

1. Corn husks should be peeled back but kept at the bottom attached. Fold the husks back up over the corn after removing the silks. Cook the corn for 5 minutes on High power, flipping it once halfway through, on a dinner plate. Corn kernels should be cut from the cob and placed in a serving bowl after cooling until they are cool enough to touch.
2. Butter, tomatoes, jalapenos, red onions, garlic, and cilantro should all be mixed into the corn. Add spice blend, salt, and pepper to taste. Mix thoroughly, taste, and, if necessary, adjust the seasoning. Although I like to serve the salad slightly chilled, some people prefer it warm.

Scalloped Potatoes

Serve: 6|Time: 25 minutes

Cal| 166 Fat|4.9 g Protein| 4.1 g Fiber| 3.7g Cholesterol | 14 mg

Ingredients

- ❖ 4 potatoes, peeled and sliced
- ❖ 30 g chopped onion
- ❖ 30 g butter
- ❖ 30 g coconut flour
- ❖ 8g salt
- ❖ 350 ml coconut milk
- ❖ 2 g dried parsley, or to taste (Optional)

Directions

1. Combine the potatoes, onion, and butter in a big dish that can be used in the microwave.
2. Combine the flour and salt in a bowl. The potatoes should then be lightly coated after being sprinkled with this mixture.
3. Pour milk on top of the potatoes.
4. Microwave potatoes for approximately 15 minutes on high, stirring every five minutes.
5. Five minutes before serving, cover the potatoes with parsley and paprika and set them aside.

Lime Cilantro Cauliflower "Rice"

Serve: 4|Time: 25 minutes

Cal| 92 Fat| 5.9 g Protein| 1.5 g Fiber| 2.2 g Cholesterol | 15 mg

Ingredients

- ❖ 575 g cauliflower, cut into florets
- ❖ 15 ml water
- ❖ 1 lime, juiced and zested
- ❖ 8 g chopped cilantro
- ❖ 30 g butter (Optional)

Directions

1. Once the cauliflower florets resemble rice, grate them or pulse them in a food processor.
2. In a covered dish that is microwave-safe, combine grated cauliflower and water.
3. Cook cauliflower in the microwave on high for 7 minutes or until it is soft.
4. Cauliflower that has been cooked with butter should also be thoroughly mixed with lime juice, zest, and cilantro.

Steamy Zucchini

Serve: 4|Time: 25 minutes

Cal| 86 Fat| 5 g Protein| 5.7 g Fiber| 1.8 g Cholesterol | 15 mg

Ingredients

- ❖ 390 g zucchini, sliced
- ❖ 80 g stalks celery, chopped
- ❖ 70 g onion, chopped
- ❖ 70 g large fresh mushrooms, sliced
- ❖ 60 g shredded Cheddar cheese

Directions

1. In a dish that can go in the microwave, combine the zucchini, celery, onion, and mushrooms. Dish with plastic wrap on it.
2. About 6 minutes on High should be enough time to steam and just barely soften the vegetables.
3. When you have finished stirring the veggies and adding the Cheddar cheese, remove the plastic wrap from the dish and replace it tightly. Allow the dish to sit for 2 to 3 minutes so the cheese can melt. To evenly distribute the melted cheese, stir the vegetables.

Baked Sweet Potatoes

Serve:2|Time: 25 minutes

Cal| 319 Fat| 11.8 g Protein| 2.6 g Fiber| 8 g Cholesterol | 31 mg

Ingredients

- ❖ 260 g sweet potatoes
- ❖ 30 g unsalted butter
- ❖ 15 ml honey
- ❖ 15 g ground cinnamon
- ❖ 4 g salt

Directions

1. With a fork, prick the sweet potatoes several times all over after washing.
2. Put the object in the microwave, on top of a paper towel, then cover it with yet another towel. 5 minutes on high in the oven (may need more depending on strength of the microwave and thickness of the potato).
3. Flip the potatoes over and cook for an additional five minutes. Test for softness after removing the potatoes. If not soft, cook for an additional 1 to 2 minutes. Potatoes should cool for one to two minutes after being wrapped in aluminium foil.
4. Open them up, then add salt, honey, cinnamon, and butter. With a fork, mash the tender meat.

Dinner Recipes

Potato Soup

Serve:12|Time: 30 minutes

Cal| 327 Fat| 16.8 g Protein| 10.1 g Fiber| 3.6 g Cholesterol | 47 mg

Ingredients

- ❖ 8 potatoes, peeled and cubed
- ❖ 110 g butter
- ❖ 62 g coconut flour
- ❖ 1900 ml coconut milk
- ❖ 28 g chopped onion
- ❖ 225 g sour cream
- ❖ 56 g shredded Cheddar cheese
- ❖ salt and pepper to taste

Directions

1. In a glass dish, add cubed potatoes, and microwave for 7 to 10 minutes, or until tender.
2. Melt the butter in a sizable pot over medium-high heat as the potatoes cook. Stir in the milk gradually after whisking in the flour until it's smooth. Bring to a boil, lower the heat to medium, and simmer for five to ten minutes, or until the mixture is just beginning to thicken.
3. After adding the potatoes and onion, simmer for a further five minutes. Sour cream and Cheddar cheese should be thoroughly combined after being added. Add salt and pepper to taste.

Cheesy Tuna and Noodels

Serve: 2|Time: 10 minutes

Cal| 177 Fat| 6.5 g Protein| 16.6 g Fiber| 0.5 g Cholesterol | 12.3 mg

Ingredients

- ❖ 250 ml boiling water
- ❖ 85 g egg ramen noodles
- ❖ 85 g water-packed tuna, drained
- ❖ 2 slices goat cheese

Directions

1. Water should be placed in a microwave-safe bowl and heated for two minutes on high power. Add the ramen noodles and cook them in the microwave for a further two minutes.
2. Noodles should be drained and their water discarded before adding seasoning, tuna, and American cheese. Place back into the microwave and heat for an additional one to two minutes. Before serving, stir.

Cheesy Tuna and Noodles

Serve: 2|Time: 10 minutes

Cal| 177 Fat| 6.5 g Protein| 16.6 g Fiber| 0.5 g Cholesterol | 12.3 mg

Ingredients

- ❖ 250 ml boiling water
- ❖ 85 g egg ramen noodles
- ❖ 85 g water-packed tuna, drained
- ❖ 2 slices goat cheese

Directions

1. Water should be placed in a microwave-safe bowl and heated for two minutes on high power. Add the ramen noodles and cook them in the microwave for a further two minutes.
2. Noodles should be drained and their water discarded before adding seasoning, tuna, and goat cheese. Place back into the microwave and heat for an additional one to two minutes. Before serving, stir.

Poached Salmon

Serve: 4|Time: 20 minutes

Cal| 356 Fat| 22.6 g Protein| 34.9 g Fiber| 0.1 g Cholesterol | 109 mg

Ingredients

- ❖ 56 ml coconut oil
- ❖ 25 ml apple cider vinegar
- ❖ 15 ml lime juice
- ❖ 15 g dried thyme
- ❖ 4 g coconut sugar
- ❖ salt and ground black pepper to taste
- ❖ 700 g salmon fillets

Directions

1. In a microwave-safe container, combine the coconut oil, apple cider vinegar, lime juice, dried thyme, coconut sugar, salt, and black pepper. The plate is shielded.
2. Microwave the oil mixture for 45 to 60 seconds to melt it. Add the salmon to the butter mixture with the skin side facing up, then seal the pan. In the microwave, cook the salmon for about 6 minutes, or until it flakes easily.

Pulled Pork Burritos

Serve: 8|Time: 25 minutes

Cal| 395 Fat| 17.4g Protein| 21.3 g Fiber| 5.2 g Cholesterol | 52 mg

Ingredients

- ❖ 450 g baked beans
- ❖ 8 (10 inches) almond flour tortillas
- ❖ 70 g onion, diced
- ❖ 450 g cooked pulled beef, heated
- ❖ 220 g shredded goat cheese
- ❖ 450 g tomato sauce

Directions

1. Pour the beans into a saucepan and boil them there over low heat.
2. Arrange a tortilla on a microwave-safe tray, then add an onion, 30 g of beans, and 4 g of pulled meat on top. Before rolling the tortilla, add goat cheese. 45 g of tomato sauce and additional cheese should be added to the meal.
3. The cheese will melt entirely in the microwave in around 1 minute. With the other tortillas and filler ingredients, repeat the process.

Avocado Corn Salad

Serve: 6|Time: 20 minutes

Cal| 265 Fat| 20.4g Protein| 3.3 g Fiber| 6.3 g Cholesterol | 0 mg

Ingredients

- ❖ 328 g fresh corn in husks
- ❖ 341 g cherry tomatoes, halved
- ❖ 2 medium avocados, diced
- ❖ 30 g chopped fresh cilantro

Dressing:

- ❖ 45 ml vegetable oil
- ❖ 15 g honey
- ❖ 28 ml lime juice
- ❖ 1 clove garlic, minced
- ❖ freshly cracked black pepper to taste

Directions

1. Microwave the ears of corn for 5 to 6 minutes on high power or until they are soft.
2. Tomatoes and avocados should be combined in a sizable mixing dish. Cut the corn kernels from the cobs and place them in the bowl. Stir in the cilantro after adding it.
3. Over the vegetable mixture, combine the oil, honey, lime juice, garlic, and black pepper. Throw and plate.

Cheesy Chicken and Rice Casserole

Serve: 5|Time: 45 minutes

Cal| 600 Fat| 19.9 g Protein| 37.3 g Fiber| 1.5 g Cholesterol | 102 mg

Ingredients

- 450 g skinless, boneless chicken breast halves - cut into bite size pieces
- salt and pepper to taste
- 370 g cooked white rice
- 280 ml condensed cream of chicken soup
- 220 g shredded Cheddar cheese
- 3 slices soft white bread, cubed

Directions

1. Set oven to 350 degrees Fahrenheit (175 degrees C).
2. Chicken should be seasoned with salt and pepper to taste, placed in a dish made for the microwave, covered, and cooked there for 5 to 6 minutes. Cook for a further 2 to 3 minutes, or until the inside is cooked through and no longer pink. Cool down.
3. Chicken, rice, and soup should all be combined thoroughly in a 9 x 13 inch baking dish. Add cheese, then bread cubes, to the top.
4. For 20 minutes, bake at 350 degrees F (175 degrees C), or until the bread is crisp and the cheese is melted and bubbling.

Cauliflower with Dijon Sauce

Serve: 4 |Time: 15 minutes

Cal| 255 Fat| 19.9 g Protein| 9.3 g Fiber| 2.2 g Cholesterol | 37 mg

Ingredients

- ❖ 265 g cauliflower, separated into florets
- ❖ 120 g mayonnaise
- ❖ 60 g Dijon mustard
- ❖ 110 g shredded sharp Cheddar cheese

Directions

1. Cover a large glass bowl or casserole dish with plastic wrap after adding the cauliflower florets. Use a knife to make a few small slits in the plastic. Cook for 5 to 7 minutes in the microwave, or until tender.
2. You should combine the mayonnaise and Dijon mustard in a cup or small basin. Cover the cauliflower's top with the mixture. Shredded cheese should be added on top. Return to the microwave and heat for 2 minutes, or just until the cheese has melted.

Buttery Lemon Spinach

Serye: 6 |Time: 10 minutes

Cal| 122 Fat| 9.7 g Protein| 2.5 g Fiber| 2.3 g Cholesterol | 25 mg

Ingredients

- ❖ 560 pre-washed fresh spinach
- ❖ 30 g garlic, minced
- ❖ 75 g butter
- ❖ 30 ml lemon juice

Directions

1. After rinsing, put the spinach on a plate that can be microwaved. Lemon juice, butter, and garlic are added. Wrap with plastic to protect. About 2 minutes of microwave steaming is required to wilt the spinach and melt the butter.
2. Before serving, take the plastic wrap off and toss to evenly distribute the spice.

Cheesy Cauliflower

Serve: 4 |Time: 25 minutes

Cal| 122 Fat| 9.7 g Protein| 2.5 g Fiber| 2.3 g Cholesterol | 25 mg

Ingredients

- ❖ 575 g head cauliflower, separated into florets
- ❖ butter-flavoured cooking spray
- ❖ 1 g salt, or to taste
- ❖ Pinch of ground black pepper
- ❖ 8 g Italian-style bread crumbs
- ❖ 7 g freshly grated Parmesan cheese
- ❖ 3 cloves garlic, minced, or more to taste
- ❖ 1 g red pepper flakes (Optional)

Directions

1. Put the cauliflower in a bowl that can be used in the microwave, then wrap it in paper towels. Cook for 5 to 6 minutes on high in the microwave. Cauliflower should be taken out of the microwave, and any liquid drained and stirred. Return to the microwave and cook for an additional 5 to 6 minutes, or until soft.
2. Cooking spray with a butter taste should be used to coat cauliflower before salting and peppering it. Garlic, Parmesan cheese, and bread crumbs should be added and combined.
3. 1 to 2 more minutes in the microwave will get the cheese melted.

Sesame Udon Noodles

Serve: 4 |Time: 25 minutes

Cal| 462 Fat| 27.4 g Protein| 11.1 g Fiber| 5.5 g Cholesterol | 0 mg

Ingredients

- ❖ 5 g garlic powder
- ❖ 15 g   ginger powder
- ❖ 60 g coconut amions
- ❖ 45 ml apple cider vinegar
- ❖ 55 g coconut oil
- ❖ 45 ml sesame oil
- ❖ 1 dash hot sauce

- ❖ 80 g green bell pepper, julienned
- ❖ 80 g red bell pepper, julienned
- ❖ 80 g yellow bell pepper, julienned
- ❖ 60 g green onions, minced
- ❖ 285 g diagonally sliced snap peas
- ❖ 30 g sesame seeds, toasted
- ❖ 200 g fresh udon noodles

Directions

1. Put the ginger powder, coconut oil, apple cider vinegar, coconut aminos, and spicy pepper sauce in a bottle with a tight-fitting lid. Shake ferociously to integrate after securing the cover. Set them aside to allow the flavours to mingle.
2. In a big saucepan, heat up a lot of water. Add the udon noodles and cook for three minutes, or until soft. Drain, then put in a serving bowl.
3. Put peas, green onions, and bell peppers in a bowl that can go in the microwave. meal till warm yet crispy in the microwave. Add to the bowl of noodles, then cover everything with the dressing. Add the toasted sesame seeds on top after tossing to evenly distribute the dressing.

Macaroni and Cheese

Serve: 4 |Time: 30 minutes

Cal| 691 Fat| 40.6 g Protein| 31 g Fiber| 2 g Cholesterol | 129 mg

Ingredients

- ❖ 225 g macaroni
- ❖ 30 g butter
- ❖ 25 g chopped onion
- ❖ 450 g cubed processed cheese food

- ❖ 160 ml milk
- ❖ salt to taste
- ❖ ground black pepper to taste

Directions

1. A large saucepan of salted water should be brought to a boil. For 8 to 10 minutes, cook macaroni pasta in boiling water until it's al dente. Drain then set apart.
2. Cook on high in the microwave for 3 to 4 minutes with the butter and onions in a 2-quart covered casserole dish that is microwave-safe.
3. Stir in the pasta, cheese cubes, and milk in the casserole dish. Cook for 11 to 12 minutes in the microwave on high, stirring well after 4, 8, and 11 minutes. At this point, the mixture will still be watery. Add salt and pepper to taste.
4. Before serving, let stand for 5 to 8 minutes; the sauce will thicken as it cools.

Asparagus Soup

Serve: 4 |Time: 35 minutes

Cal| 120 Fat| 6.9 g Protein| 6.1 g Fiber| 3 g Cholesterol | 19 mg

Ingredients

- ❖ 110 g onion, chopped
- ❖ 30 g butter
- ❖ 450 g fresh asparagus, trimmed and coarsely chopped
- ❖ 250 ml vegetable broth
- ❖ 1 dash garlic powder
- ❖ 1 dash white pepper
- ❖ 250 ml coconut milk

Directions

1. 2 minutes on HIGH in the microwave with the onion and butter. Include the vegetable broth, asparagus, garlic powder, and white pepper. 10 to 12 minutes on HIGH in a covered microwave. Blend in a blender.
2. Return the mixture to a dish that can be heated in the microwave, stir in the milk, and heat through.

Lemon Pepper Dill Fish

Serye: 4 |Time: 20 minutes

Cal| 333 Fat| 24.2 g Protein| 27.8 g Fiber| 0.1 g Cholesterol | 145 mg

Ingredients

- ❖ 450 g haddock fillets
- ❖ 115 g butter
- ❖ dried dill weed to taste
- ❖ lemon pepper to taste
- ❖ 45 ml fresh lemon juice

Directions

1. Put fish fillets on a dish that can go in the microwave. Put butter on the fish in chunks and sprinkle it all over. Add some lemon pepper and dill weed. Fresh lemon juice should be poured all over the fish.
2. For 3 to 5 minutes on high, with the lid on, cook the fish until it turns white.

Stuffed Acorn Squash

Serve: 4 |Time: 30 minutes

Cal| 113 Fat| 4.6 g Protein| 4.5 g Fiber| 2.7 g Cholesterol | 13 mg

Ingredients

- 170 g package broccoli and cheese flavoured rice mix
- 450 g turkey breakfast sausage
- 430 g acorn squash, halved and seeded
- 60 g chopped apple
- 10 g crushed coriander seed
- 55 g shredded Monterey Jack cheese

Directions

1. Follow the instructions on the rice mix container for preparation; cover and set away.
2. Squash halves should be placed cut side down on a plate. When the squash is soft but firm, cook it in the microwave on High for 5 minutes.
3. Sausage should be cooked until it is evenly browned in a medium skillet over medium heat. Drain and set aside.
4. Combine the cooked rice, sausage, apple, and coriander in a sizable bowl. Stuff the mixture into each squash half.
5. The squash should be heated in the microwave for about 5 minutes, with the plastic wrap still on the squash halves. Remove the wrap, then sprinkle cheese on the packed squash. Cooking should continue for about a minute or until the cheese is melted.

Garlic-and-Herb Green Beans

Serve: 6 |Time: 20 minutes

Cal| 46 Fat| 2.4g Protein| 1.5 g Fiber| 2.6 g Cholesterol | 0 mg

Ingredients

- ❖ 450 g fresh green beans, trimmed
- ❖ 125 g water, or more as needed
- ❖ 3 cloves garlic, minced

- ❖ 15 ml extra-virgin olive oil
- ❖ 2 g dried basil
- ❖ salt and ground black pepper to taste

Directions

1. Put green beans in a glass dish that can go in the microwave. Mix in the water, oil, garlic, basil, salt, and pepper. Put a lid on the dish.
2. 5 minutes at high power in the microwave.
3. Stir the green beans and check the water level, adding more if necessary. After 3 to 5 minutes, replace the lid and microwave the food until it's tender-crisp.

Pasta Salad

Serve: 2 |Time: 10 minutes

Cal| 1024 Fat| 18.6g Protein| 37.6 g Fiber| 9 g Cholesterol | 40 mg

Ingredients

- ❖ 450 g Pasta Penne
- ❖ 180 g red and yellow cherry tomatoes
- ❖ 60 g Italian dressing
- ❖ Basil, shredded
- ❖ Salt and pepper to taste
- ❖ 30 g Parmigiano-Reggiano cheese

Directions

1. To vent, rip a corner off the Ready Pasta packet. Microwave for one minute.
2. Pasta should be mixed with chopped tomatoes, Italian dressing, and basil.
3. Add cheese and season with salt and pepper.

Garlic Green Beans

Serve: 4 |Time: 10 minutes

Cal| 46 Fat| 3g Protein| 1.2 g Fiber| 2 g Cholesterol | 8 mg

Ingredients

- ❖ 225 g fresh green beans, trimmed
- ❖ 60 ml water
- ❖ 15 g butter
- ❖ 15 g minced garlic
- ❖ 15 g chicken bouillon granules

Directions

1. Green beans should be cooked in a microwave-safe bowl with water until they are soft, about 5 minutes on high. Drain.
2. Combine the beans with the butter, garlic, and chicken bouillon.

Garlic Chicken

Serve: 4 |Time: 20 minutes

Cal| 360 Fat| 28.3g Protein| 25.5 g Fiber| 0.3 g Cholesterol | 128 mg

Ingredients

- ❖ 500 ml water
- ❖ 2 cubes chicken bouillon
- ❖ 115 g butter
- ❖ 15 g dried Italian seasoning (Optional)

- ❖ 2 g dried dill weed (Optional)
- ❖ 4 g garlic salt, or to taste
- ❖ 450 g chicken breast halves, both skinless and boneless

Directions

1. A casserole dish made for the microwave should be filled with water before being placed inside. Heat for about 2 minutes, or until boiling. Add the bouillon cubes, butter, dill, garlic salt, and Italian seasoning.
2. Place the punctured side of the chicken breasts in the casserole dish after scoring them with a fork on one side. If not entirely, the liquid should be almost totally covering the chicken.
3. Cook the food for 10 minutes in the microwave, or until the chicken is no longer pink and the liquids are clear. Cook the chicken for a further 10 minutes, checking it every 10 minutes, at 1 1/2 minute intervals.

Lemon Pepper Peas

Serve: 4 |Time: 10 minutes

Cal| 108 Fat| 6g Protein| 3.9 g Fiber| 3.6 g Cholesterol | 10.3 mg

Ingredients

- ❖ 280 g package frozen green peas, thawed
- ❖ 15 ml water
- ❖ 30 g butter
- ❖ 1 pinch lemon pepper
- ❖ 1 pinch dried dill weed

Directions

1. In a bowl that can go in the microwave, put the peas and water. When the peas are cooked, microwave for 3 to 4 minutes with a loose cover. Add butter, then top with dill and lemon pepper. Serve hot.

Baked Potato with Mushrooms

Serve: 1 |Time: 45 minutes

Cal| 397 Fat| 12.4 g Protein| 9.5 g Fiber| 9.8 g Cholesterol | 32 mg

Ingredients

- ❖ 1 large baking potato
- ❖ 15 g unsalted butter
- ❖ 40 g chopped onions
- ❖ 35 g chopped mushrooms
- ❖ salt to taste
- ❖ 30 g coconut yogurt

Directions

1. Set the oven to 450 degrees Fahrenheit (230 degrees C).
2. Use a fork to lightly pierce the potato. Cook for 10 minutes on high in the microwave, stirring once or twice, until soft but not mushy. Bake the potato for 15 minutes in a preheated oven after transferring it to a baking dish.
3. Butter should be melted in a pan over medium heat. Mix in the onion. until tender, cook and stir. Add the mushrooms. Use salt to season. Once the mushrooms are soft, turn the heat down to low, cover the pan, and wait 5 minutes. Potato should be served with yoghurt and mushrooms on top.

Side Dishes

Potato Chips

Serve: 4 |Time: 35 minutes

Cal| 80 Fat| 3.5 g Protein|1.5 g Fiber| 1.1 g Cholesterol | 32 mg

Ingredients

- ❖ 15 ml olive oil
- ❖ 1 potato, sliced
- ❖ 2 g salt, or to taste

Directions

1. Put the olive oil in a bag made of plastic (a produce bag works well). Shake to coat the potato slices after adding them.
2. Apply a thin layer of oil or frying spray to a large dinner plate. On the dish, arrange the potato slices in a single layer.
3. Cook for 3 to 5 minutes in the microwave, or until gently browned (if not browned, they will not become crisp). Depending on the strength of your microwave, times will change. Take the chips off the dish and season with salt (or other seasonings). Cool down. With the remaining potato slices, repeat the process.

Corn on the Cob

Serve: 1 |Time: 05 minutes

Cal| 122 Fat| 1.5 g Protein|4.5 g Fiber| 3.8 g Cholesterol | 32 mg

Ingredients

❖ 1 fresh corn

Directions

1. Take the silk and husk from the corn ear.
2. Dampen a paper towel, wring it out, and keep it damp. The ear of corn should be wrapped in a wet towel and set on a dish that can be used in a microwave.
3. Cook in the microwave for 3 to 5 minutes, or until the kernels are soft but still hold their shape when tested with a knife.
4. Before serving, carefully remove and discard the paper towel.

Popcorn

Serve: 2 |Time: 10 minutes

Cal| 114 Fat| 3.5 g Protein|3 g Fiber| 3.8 g Cholesterol | 32 mg

Ingredients

- ❖ 240 g unpopped popcorn
- ❖ salt to taste
- ❖ 4 g olive oil, or more if needed

Directions

1. Put popcorn in a bag made of brown paper. Fold the top of the bag many times to create a tight closure.
2. About 2 minutes of high-speed microwave cooking should stop the popping. Open the bag slowly. Olive oil should be drizzled and salt added. After shaking to disperse the seasoning, reseal the bag.

Baked Apples

Serve: 2 |Time: 10 minutes

Cal| 114 Fat| 3.5 g Protein|3 g Fiber| 3.8 g Cholesterol | 32 mg

Ingredients

- ❖ 2 apples
- ❖ 30 g brown sugar
- ❖ 4 g ground cinnamon
- ❖ 4 g ground nutmeg
- ❖ 10 g butter

Directions

1. When coring apples, leave the bottom alone.
2. In a bowl, combine brown sugar, cinnamon, and nutmeg. Place one teaspoon of butter on top of each apple after spooning half of the sugar mixture into each one. Put apples in a large casserole dish that can be microwaved, then cover.
3. 3 1/2 to 4 minutes in the microwave until soft. Before serving, give apples two minutes to sit.

Jalapeno Popper Spread

Serve: 32 |Time: 13 minutes

Cal| 93 Fat| 7.8 g Protein|1.8 g Fiber| 1.1 g Cholesterol | 18 mg

Ingredients

- ❖ 450 g Greek yogurt,
- ❖ 250 g mayonnaise
- ❖ 110 g can be chopped cayenne pepper, drained
- ❖ 60 g canned Serrano Peppers, drained
- ❖ 30 g grated mozzarella cheese

Directions

1. In a sizable bowl, combine Greek yogurt, and mayonnaise and stir until combined. Add Serrano pepper and cayenne pepper after stirring. Place mixture in a serving bowl that can be used in the microwave, then top with mozzarella cheese.
2. Heat in the microwave for about 3 minutes on High.

Caramel Popcorn

Serve: 16 |Time: 15 minutes

Cal| 130 Fat| 6 g Protein|1.1 g Fiber| 1.2 g Cholesterol | 0 mg

Ingredients

- ❖ 900 g popped popcorn
- ❖ 240 g brown sugar
- ❖ 50 g margarine
- ❖ 75 g light corn syrup
- ❖ 2 g salt
- ❖ 4 g vanilla extract
- ❖ 2 g baking soda

Directions

1. Put the popped popcorn in a sizable bag made of brown paper. Place aside.
2. Mix the brown sugar, margarine, corn syrup, salt, and vanilla in a 2-quart casserole dish or other heat-resistant glass dish. In the microwave, heat for three minutes, then remove and mix until thoroughly combined. Once more, heat for 1 1/2 minutes in the microwave. After removing it from the microwave, add the baking soda.
3. Drizzle syrup over the bagged popcorn. Close the bag by rolling the top down once or twice, then shake to coat the corn. Cook the bag for 1 minute and 10 seconds in the microwave. Return the bag to the microwave after shaking, removing, and turning it over. Cook for a further 1 min. 10 sec. Put the popcorn on wax paper, then let it cool until the coating is hardened. Use an airtight container for storage.

Soft-Boiled Eggs

Serve:2 |Time: 10 minutes

Cal| 63 Fat| 4.4 g Protein|5.5 g Fiber| 0 g Cholesterol | 164 mg

Ingredients

- ❖ water
- ❖ 2 eggs
- ❖ 2 g salt

Directions

1. To prevent breaking when you boil the eggs, put cold eggs into a bowl of warm water.
2. Add salt to a dish of water that can be heated in a microwave. To boil, use a high power microwave for 1 to 1 1/2 minutes.
3. Put the warm eggs into the hot water in the bowl and wrap the bowl in plastic.
4. Put the covered bowl of eggs in the microwave and cook for 1 1/2 minutes at 60% power.
5. Eggs should be taken out of the microwave and placed in a bowl of cool water to stop cooking. Peel, then dish.

Easy Buffalo Chicken Dip

Serve:20 |Time: 15 minutes

Cal| 144 Fat| 7.7 g Protein|10.4 g Fiber| 1.1 g Cholesterol | 39 mg

Ingredients

- ❖ 570 g Pulled Chicken Breast, thawed
- ❖ 225 g package cream cheese, softened
- ❖ 240 g sour cream
- ❖ 120 g Buffalo sauce
- ❖ 340 g package tortilla chips

Directions

1. Buffalo sauce, sour cream, and cream cheese should all be combined in a mixing or microwave-safe bowl.
2. After the pulled chicken has defrosted, fold it in. You may serve the dip cold or reheat it in the microwave for two minutes on high while stirring.
3. Serve with your preferred tortilla chips in

Easy Cheese Dip

Serve:4 |Time: 06 minutes

Cal| 189 Fat| 17.7 g Protein|6.2 g Fiber| 0 g Cholesterol | 53 mg

Ingredients

- ❖ 116 g cream cheese
- ❖ 60 g sour cream
- ❖ 60 g shredded aged Cheddar cheese

Directions

1. In a bowl that can be heated in the microwave, combine the cream cheese and sour cream. Microwave for about 30 seconds, or until the mixture is soft and easy to stir.
2. Stirring Cheddar cheese into the cream cheese mixture, heat in the microwave for 30 to 40 seconds, or until the dip is smooth. Stir. If more heating is required, microwave for another 10 seconds.

Pumpkin Spice Latte

Serve:1 |Time: 05 minutes

Cal| 189 Fat| 17.7 g Protein|6.2 g Fiber| 0 g Cholesterol | 53 mg

Ingredients

- ❖ 30 ml half-and-half
- ❖ 10 g white sugar, or to taste
- ❖ 1 g pumpkin pie spice
- ❖ 240 g coffee
- ❖ 15 g whipped cream topping, or to taste (Optional)

Directions

1. In a coffee mug, combine half-and-half, sugar, and pumpkin pie spice. Add coffee to mug and stir to combine.
2. Microwave for about 15 seconds or until heated. Add whipped cream over top.

Strawberry Cheesecake Bites

Serve:12 |Time: 45 minutes

Cal| 101 Fat| 7.1 g Protein|1.6 g Fiber| 0.4 g Cholesterol | 21mg

Ingredients

- ❖ 225 g cream cheese
- ❖ 120 g confectioners' sugar
- ❖ 8 g vanilla extract
- ❖ 12 large fresh strawberries, hulled
- ❖ 30 g graham cracker crumbs
- ❖ 60 g squares semisweet chocolate chips (Optional)
- ❖ 4 g canola oil (Optional)

Directions

1. Using wax paper, cover a baking sheet.
2. Cream cheese, confectioners' sugar, and vanilla essence are combined and smoothed out in a bowl.
3. Fill a piping bag with the mixture and attach a large round tip.
4. Cut a cone-shaped hole in the top of each strawberry with a sharp paring knife to create a little hollow.

1. Fill each strawberry with about 1 spoonful of the cream cheese filling, making sure that some of the fillings spills over the top.
5. In a small bowl, add the graham cracker crumbs. To cover the exposed filling with crumbs, dip the filled side of the strawberry into the graham cracker crumbs.
6. In a glass or ceramic bowl that can be used in the microwave, melt the chocolate and canola oil in 30-second intervals, stirring after each one, until warm and smooth, 1 to 3 minutes (depending on your microwave).
7. Placed on the prepared baking sheet, the strawberry's empty ends are dipped into the melted chocolate and chilled until firm.

Cinnamon Apples

Serve:4 |Time: 10 minutes

Cal| 62 Fat| 0.2 g Protein|0.3 g Fiber| 2.9 g Cholesterol | 0mg

Ingredients

- ❖ 2 apples, diced
- ❖ 4 g white sugar
- ❖ 2 g ground cinnamon

Directions

1. Apples should be heated for 30 seconds in a microwave-safe bowl. Apples are covered with sugar and cinnamon, which are then stirred in. Apples should be microwaved for an additional minute or so until mushy and toasty.

Easy Glazed Carrots

Serve:4 |Time: 10 minutes

Cal| 265 Fat| 11.5 g Protein|1.1 g Fiber| 2.9 g Cholesterol | 31 mg

Ingredients

- ❖ 450 g sliced carrots, drained
- ❖ 145 g brown sugar
- ❖ 100g butter
- ❖ 30 ml orange marmalade

Directions

1. Brown sugar, butter, and orange marmalade should all be added to a microwave-safe bowl of carrots. Wrap some plastic wrap loosely around the bowl.
2. Stir after three minutes of cooking on high in the microwave. If the butter and marmalade aren't fully melted, cook on high in increments of 30 seconds, stirring after each one, until the carrots are covered in glaze.

Cornbread

Serve: 6 |Time: 10 minutes

Cal| 152 Fat| 6.2 g Protein|3.5 g Fiber| 1.1 g Cholesterol | 29 mg

Ingredients

- ❖ 120 g almond flour
- ❖ 120 g cornmeal
- ❖ 30 g coconut sugar
- ❖ 8 g baking powder
- ❖ 1 g salt
- ❖ 1 egg
- ❖ 100 ml milk
- ❖ 30 ml vegetable oil

Directions

1. Combine the cornmeal, almond flour, baking powder, coconut sugar salt, egg, milk, and vegetable oil in a glass or ceramic bowl that can resist the microwave.
2. Cook for about 3 minutes on high in the microwave, or until a wooden skewer in the center comes out clear. In the absence of a rotating tray in your microwave, turn the bowl halfway through heating.

Spiced Nuts

Serve: 12 |Time: 12 minutes

Cal| 152 Fat| 6.2 g Protein|3.5 g Fiber| 1.1 g Cholesterol | 29 mg

Ingredients

- ❖ 50 g butter
- ❖ 120 g brown sugar
- ❖ 2 g ground nutmeg
- ❖ 4 g ground cinnamon
- ❖ 30 ml water
- ❖ 375 g pecan halves

Directions

1. In a 4-quart glass casserole dish, microwave butter until it is melted. Add the water, nutmeg, cinnamon, and brown sugar by stirring. The microwave should be on high for one minute.
2. Add the nuts and stir until thoroughly coated. Stirring every minute, continue to microwave for an additional 4 to 5 minutes on high. To cool, spread out cooked nuts on parchment or waxed paper.

Hot Chocolate

Serve: 1 |Time: 10 minutes

Cal| 248 Fat| 7.1 g Protein|9.1 g Fiber| 1.3 g Cholesterol | 20 mg

Ingredients

- ❖ 250 ml milk
- ❖ 45 g instant hot chocolate mix
- ❖ 4 g ground cinnamon
- ❖ 1 pinch cayenne pepper

Directions

1. In a mug, combine the hot chocolate mix, cinnamon, and cayenne pepper.
2. Pour the milk into a glass measuring cup and heat it in the microwave on High for about 2 minutes, or until it starts to boil. Pour contents into mug slowly, whisking with a tiny whisk as you do so. Enjoy right away.

Peanut Butter Popcorn

Serve: 8|Time: 15 minutes

Cal| 200 Fat| 14.1 g Protein|2.2 g Fiber| 0.5 g Cholesterol | 0 mg

Ingredients

- ❖ 200g packages microwave popcorn, popped
- ❖ 120 g margarine
- ❖ 150 g brown sugar
- ❖ 50 g peanut butter
- ❖ 20 large marshmallows

Directions

1. Put the popcorn in a sizable bowl.
2. Combine margarine, brown sugar, and marshmallows in a bowl that can be heated in a microwave. Stirring in between each 1-minute interval, cook the mixture in the microwave until it is melted and smooth. Once everything is well combined, add the peanut butter..
3. Sprinkle the popcorn with the brown sugar mixture and immediately toss to coat it before it cools.

Chinese Noodle Salad

Serve: 8|Time: 5 minutes

Cal| 151 Fat| 8.8 g Protein|1.9 g Fiber| 1 g Cholesterol | 6 mg

Ingredients

- 60 ml rice vinegar
- 50 g sugar
- 60 ml vegetable oil
- 170 g ramen noodles with seasoning packet
- ½ head romaine lettuce, chopped
- 280 g mandarin orange segments, drained
- 35 g slivered almonds

Directions

1. Combine vinegar, sugar, and oil in a bowl that can be heated in the microwave. One minute on high in the microwave will get the sugar to dissolve. Well , combine, then set aside to cool.
2. In the packages, crush the ramen noodles. Add to the salad dressing.
3. Combine romaine lettuce, oranges, almonds, and salad dressing in a bowl.

Curried Cauliflower

Serve: 4|Time: 20 minutes

Cal| 94 Fat| 5.6 g Protein|3.3 g Fiber| 2.7 g Cholesterol | 5 mg

Ingredients

- ❖ 575 g cauliflower
- ❖ 60 g light mayonnaise
- ❖ 60 g plain Greek yogurt
- ❖ 30 g curry powder, or more to taste

Directions

1. Cauliflower should be cored, leaving enough of the core to keep it intact.

1. Curry powder, Greek yogurt, and mayonnaise are combined in a bowl.
2. Spread the curry mixture over the cauliflower head, then put it in a large bowl that can be heated in the microwave and cover it with a plate.
3. Cook cauliflower in the microwave on High for 9 to 15 minutes, or until it is soft; cover and let stand for another 2 minutes.
4. Slice into quarters, then serve.

Zucchini Chip Nachos

Serve: 2|Time: 10 minutes

Cal| 329 Fat| 20.7 g Protein|16.9 g Fiber| 3.6 g Cholesterol | 59 mg

Ingredients

- ❖ 320 g zucchini, sliced
- ❖ cooking spray
- ❖ 30 g taco seasoning mix
- ❖ 30 g sliced black olives
- ❖ 30 g chopped red onion
- ❖ 8 slices pickled jalapeno pepper
- ❖ 225 g shredded Cheddar cheese

Directions

1. Cut zucchini into 1/8-inch slices using a mandoline set to the thinnest setting after trimming the ends. Slices should be placed on a platter lined with paper towels, covered with more paper towels, and pressed to absorb any extra moisture.
2. Slices of zucchini should be placed on a cutting board and given a light cooking spray mist. Slices should be turned over and seasoned with taco seasoning and lightly sprayed with cooking spray. Make sure none of the slices are overlapping as you arrange them on a microwave-safe plate, seasoning side up. Cook for 2 minutes and 30 seconds on high power in the microwave. Slices should be carefully turned over and cooked for a further 30 seconds. the remaining zucchini, and repeat.
3. On two microwave-safe plates, distribute the chips. Add Cheddar cheese, red onion, jalapeño peppers, and black olives. About 30 seconds on high power in the microwave will melt the cheese.

Dessert Recipes

Chocolaté Pudding

Serve: 4|Time: 15 minutes

Cal| 200 Fat| 3.5 g Protein|5.4 g Fiber| 2.4 g Cholesterol | 10 mg

Ingredients

- ❖ 100 g white sugar
- ❖ 35 g unsweetened cocoa powder
- ❖ 45 g corn-starch
- ❖ 500 ml coconut milk
- ❖ 8 g vanilla extract

Directions

1. Stir the sugar, cocoa, and corn-starch together in a bowl that can be heated in a microwave. To avoid any dry lumps in the mixture, whisk in the milk a bit at a time.
2. Cook for three minutes on high in the microwave. For 2 to 4 minutes, or until shiny and thick, stir, then cook at 1-minute intervals with stirring in between. Add vanilla and stir.
3. To avoid skin from forming, place a piece of plastic wrap over the pudding's surface and refrigerate. Offer chilled.

Peanut Brittle

Serve: 16|Time: 30 minutes

Cal| 92 Fat| 1.6 g Protein|0.4 g Fiber| 0.1 g Cholesterol | 2 mg

Ingredients

- ❖ 225 g dry roasted peanuts
- ❖ 200 g white sugar
- ❖ 170 g light corn syrup
- ❖ 1 pinch salt (Optional)
- ❖ 15 g butter
- ❖ 4 g vanilla extract
- ❖ 4 g baking soda

Directions

1. Set a baking sheet aside after greasing it. Combine the peanuts, sugar, corn syrup, and salt in a glass bowl. Cook combination on High (700 W) for 6 to 7 minutes or until bubbling and peanuts are browned. Add vanilla and butter; cook for a further two to three minutes.
2. Add baking soda and whisk just until froth appears. Pour right away onto an already-greased baking pan. 15 minutes or until set, let cool. Put the pieces in an airtight container after breaking them up.

Chocolate Mug Cake

Serve: 1|Time: 10 minutes

Cal| 599 Fat| 30.6 g Protein|6.9 g Fiber| 4.4 g Cholesterol | 4 mg

Ingredients

- ❖ 35 g all-purpose flour
- ❖ 50 g white sugar
- ❖ 30 g unsweetened cocoa powder
- ❖ Pinch of baking soda
- ❖ Pinch of salt

- ❖ 45 ml milk
- ❖ 30 ml canola oil
- ❖ 15 ml water
- ❖ 1 g vanilla extract

Directions

1. Combine the unsweetened cocoa powder, white sugar, baking soda, all-purpose flour, and salt in a large microwave-safe cup. Add the milk, vanilla essence, canola oil, and water.
2. Heat the cake in the microwave for 1 minute, 45 seconds, or until the middle is set.

Zucchini Bread in a Mug

Serve: 1|Time: 10 minutes

Cal| 323 Fat| 20.2 g Protein|5.5 g Fiber| 2.7 g Cholesterol | 0 mg

Ingredients

- ❖ 40 g all-purpose flour
- ❖ 20 g brown sugar
- ❖ 2 g baking powder
- ❖ 1 dash salt
- ❖ 1 g nutmeg
- ❖ 1 g vanilla extract
- ❖ 45 ml almond milk
- ❖ 10 g vegetable oil
- ❖ 45 g shredded zucchini
- ❖ 8 g chopped pecans

Directions

1. In an 8- to 12-ounce mug, combine the following ingredients: milk, brown sugar, vanilla extract, baking powder, salt, nutmeg, flour, and vegetable oil. Stir thoroughly to mix.
2. The zucchini should be dried between two paper towels. Stir in the zucchini and pecans, then finish combining the mixture.
3. Microwave unattended for 2 minutes on higher voltage. Enjoy straight from the mug.

Peanut Butter Fudge

Serve: 36|Time: 1 hr.10 minutes

Cal| 109 Fat| 9.7 g Protein|4.2 g Fiber| 9.7 g Cholesterol | 8 mg

Ingredients

- ❖ 510 g peanut butter
- ❖ 340 g whipped cream cheese frosting

Directions

1. Wax paper should be used to line an 8-inch square baking pan.
2. In a bowl that can go in the microwave, combine the peanut butter and cream cheese icing. Microwave on high for 30 seconds. Stir the mixture once more until it is fully combined, then heat it for another 30 seconds.
3. Fill the baking pan with the mixture. For about an hour, refrigerate until cool.

Chocolate Cake

Serve: 2|Time: 10 minutes

Cal| 432 Fat| 21.7 g Protein|8.5 g Fiber| 2.5 g Cholesterol | 141 mg

Ingredients

- ❖ non-stick cooking spray
- ❖ 100 g white sugar
- ❖ 90 ml milk
- ❖ 1 large egg
- ❖ 45 g butter, softened
- ❖ 4 g vanilla extract
- ❖ 70 g all-purpose flour
- ❖ 30 g cocoa powder
- ❖ 1 g baking powder
- ❖ 1 pinch salt

Directions

1. Spray non-stick cooking spray in a medium microwave-safe bowl and place it aside.
2. In a mixing dish, combine sugar, milk, egg, butter, and vanilla; thoroughly combine. In another bowl, mash together the flour, baking soda, salt, and cocoa powder. Blend the milk mixture and flour mixture until well combined. Pour into the prepared bowl that is microwave-safe.
3. Cook the cake in the microwave with the cover on for 2 to 2 1/2 minutes, or until it springs back when touched. After letting the cake cool for five minutes, place a plate over the bowl and invert the cake onto the plate.

Lemon Curd

Serve: 16|Time: 16 minutes

Cal| 116 Fat| 6.7 g Protein|1.3 g Fiber| 0.4 g Cholesterol | 46 mg

Ingredients

- ❖ 200 g white sugar
- ❖ 3 eggs
- ❖ 190 ml fresh lemon juice
- ❖ 3 lemons, zested
- ❖ 113 g unsalted butter, melted

Directions

1. Whisk the sugar and eggs until they are well combined in a bowl that can be heated in a microwave. Lemon juice, lemon zest, and butter are added. Stirring after each minute of cooking in the microwave until the sauce is thick enough to coat the back of a metal spoon. Take the food out of the microwave and place it in little, sterile jars. . Place in the refrigerator for up to three weeks.

Brownie

Serve: 1|Time: 10 minutes

Cal| 573 Fat| 29.7 g Protein|5.2 g Fiber| 4.2 g Cholesterol | 0 mg

Ingredients

- ❖ 35 g all-purpose flour
- ❖ 50 g white sugar
- ❖ 30 g cocoa powder
- ❖ 1 pinch ground cinnamon
- ❖ 1 pinch of salt
- ❖ 45 ml water
- ❖ 30 ml canola oil
- ❖ 1 splash vanilla extract

Directions

1. In a cup that can be heated in the microwave, combine the flour, sugar, cocoa powder, cinnamon, and salt. With a fork, blend the flour mixture, water, oil, and vanilla essence.
2. 1 to 5 minutes in the microwave will get it set.

Chocolate Truffle Pie

Serve: 8|Time: 8 hr. 10 minutes

Cal| 212 Fat| 11.4 g Protein|1.5 g Fiber| 2 g Cholesterol | 5 mg

Ingredients

- ❖ 340 g semisweet chocolate chips
- ❖ 22 g heavy whipping cream, divided
- ❖ 50 g sifted confectioners' sugar
- ❖ 15 g vanilla extract
- ❖ 1 prepared chocolate cookie crust

Directions

1. Chocolate chips and half the cream should be combined in a dish that can be microwaved. Stirring every 30 seconds, cook for 1 to 2 minutes on high to achieve smoothness. Until room temperature, cool. Add vanilla and sugar and stir. Place aside.
2. Beat the remaining cream in a separate basin until soft peaks form. 1/3 at a time, beat in chocolate mixture at high speed. Into the crust, spoon chocolate cream.
3. Before serving, place in the fridge for at least 8 hours.

Maple Walnut Fudge

Serve: 18|Time: 1 hr. 15 minutes

Cal| 247 Fat| 13.4 g Protein|3.5 g Fiber| 0.1 g Cholesterol | 20 mg

Ingredients

- ❖ 510 g white chocolate chips
- ❖ 400 ml sweetened condensed milk
- ❖ 60 g butter
- ❖ 4 g maple flavoured extract
- ❖ 225 g broken walnuts

Directions

1. An 8x12-inch piece of parchment paper should be used to line a greased 8x8-inch glass baking dish. The ends will protrude from the dish's side.
2. In a glass or ceramic bowl that can withstand the microwave, melt the white chocolate, sweetened condensed milk, and butter for 1 to 3 minutes, stirring after each melting (depending on your microwave). Avoid overheating chocolate since it will burn. Add the walnuts after briefly combining the maple-flavored essence. The chocolate mixture should be poured into the prepared baking dish and chilled for about an hour to set. Lift the parchment paper to reveal the fudge, then cut it into pieces.

Peanut Butter Cookie

Serve: 2|Time: 15 minutes

Cal| 212 Fat| 12.1 g Protein|6.1 g Fiber| 0.8 g Cholesterol | 97 mg

Ingredients

- ❖ 15 g butter
- ❖ 15 g peanut butter
- ❖ 15 g brown sugar
- ❖ 15 g white sugar
- ❖ 1 pinch of salt
- ❖ 1 egg
- ❖ 45 g all-purpose flour

Directions

1. Put butter and peanut butter in a mug that can go in the microwave. 30 seconds in the microwave should be enough time to melt butter and peanut butter. Add salt, white sugar, and brown sugar to the butter mixture. Add the egg, then incorporate the flour.
2. Cook in the microwave for 2 to 4 minutes, or until the cookie is set.

Banana Bread Mug Cake

Serve: 2|Time: 12 minutes

Cal| 509 Fat| 28.4 g Protein|9.9 g Fiber| 3.4 g Cholesterol | 46 mg

Ingredients

- ❖ 1 medium very ripe banana
- ❖ 45 g coconut sugar
- ❖ 1 g salt
- ❖ 1 g baking powder
- ❖ Pinch of baking soda
- ❖ 45 g melted unsalted butter
- ❖ 15 ml coconut milk

- ❖ Pinch of vanilla extract
- ❖ 70 g all-purpose flour
- ❖ 30 g chopped walnuts
- ❖ 30 g dark chocolate chips
- ❖ 6 slices of banana
- ❖ 15 g white sugar, or to taste

Directions

1. coconut milk, Banana, coconut sugar, salt, unsalted butter, baking soda and vanilla should all be combined in a mixing dish and mashed into a smooth puree. When adding the flour, only mix it in completely. Stir in the walnuts and chocolate chips.
2. Evenly pour the batter into two lightly oiled coffee cups or glasses. Give a towel and a few taps to smooth everything out and make sure there are no air pockets.
3. Microwave each cup for one minute, or until a toothpick inserted into one of them comes out clean.
4. Allow cooling before serving.
5. As a garnish, you can decide to sprinkle sugar and banana slices on top of each. Burn the tops using a blowtorch.

Caramel Pears

Serve: 5|Time: 50 minutes

Cal| 320 Fat| 14.8 g Protein| 1.9 g Fiber| 12 g Cholesterol | 0 mg

Ingredients

❖ 5 large pears

Bamboo sticks

❖ 395 g caramel sauce

❖ 30 ml water
❖ 195 g semisweet chocolate
❖ 30 g shortening, divided
❖ 240 g almond bark

Directions

1. In a large saucepan, water was boiled. pears should be rapidly dipped into hot water using a slotted spoon to dissolve any wax that may be present. After drying off, let it cool. Insert the sticks into the pears's core.
2. Waxed paper should be placed on a baking sheet and coated with cooking spray. The caramel sauce and 30 ml of water are combined in a medium microwave-safe bowl. Cook the caramel on high for 2 minutes or until it is melted and smooth, blend, and then cook and stir for another 1 minutes.
3. Apply the caramel to the pears while holding them by the stick. Place on wax paper, then chill for approximately 15 minutes to set.
4. Heat the chocolate and 15 ml of shortening in a microwave-safe bowl until completely smooth. Dip pears into chocolate to get rid of the caramel coating. Return to the wax paper to set.
5. In a microwave with the remaining shortening, melt the almond bark melts while stirring every 30 seconds. Use a fork or wooden stick to flick coloured patterns onto your apples to give them a final flourish. Keep cold for at least an entire night until set.

Banana Cake

Serve: 2|Time: 12 minutes

Cal| 223 Fat| 14.1 g Protein| 2.3 g Fiber| 0.9 g Cholesterol | 1 mg

Ingredients

- ❖ 90 g whole wheat flour
- ❖ 70 g tablespoons white sugar
- ❖ Pinch of baking powder
- ❖ ½ banana, mashed
- ❖ 45 ml coconutmilk
- ❖ 45 ml vegetable oil
- ❖ 6 g vanilla extract
- ❖ 30 g chocolate spread or to taste
  (Optional)

Directions

1. In a bowl, stir together the whole wheat flour, white sugar, and baking soda. Combine the banana, coconut milk, oil, and vanilla essence in a microwave-safe bowl. Add the flour mixture and stir once the batter is smooth.
2. Microwave the cake for two minutes, or until it is fully cooked. Once the cake has partially cooled, cover it with chocolate.

Cinnamon Muffin

Serve: 1|Time: 10 minutes

Cal| 344 Fat| 16.6 g Protein| 14.1 g Fiber| 6.2 g Cholesterol | 166 mg

Ingredients

- ❖ 1 egg
- ❖ 30 g vanilla yogurt
- ❖ 30 g chopped walnuts
- ❖ 15 g all-purpose flour
- ❖ 15 g flax seed meal

- ❖ 15 g quick-cooking oats
- ❖ 15 g honey
- ❖ 8 g ground cinnamon
- ❖ 2 g baking powder

Directions

1. In an oven-safe cup, whisk the egg. The egg should be thoroughly blended with yogurt, walnuts, flour, flax, oats, honey, cinnamon, and baking powder.
2. 90 to 100 seconds in the microwave will get it set. To get the muffin out of the mug, turn it over on a plate.

Turtles Cake

Serve: 24 |Time: 60 minutes

Cal| 344 Fat| 16.6 g Protein| 14.1 g Fiber| 6.2 g Cholesterol | 166 mg

Ingredients

- ❖ 530 g package German chocolate cake mix
- ❖ 395 g individually wrapped caramels
- ❖ 140 ml evaporated milk
- ❖ 170 g butter
- ❖ 125 g chopped pecans
- ❖ 170 g semisweet chocolate chips

Directions

1. The oven should be preheated to 350 degrees Fahrenheit (175 degrees C). Lightly grease a 9x13-inch baking dish.
2. Prepare the cake mix according to the instructions on the container. The batter should be added to the dish in less than half.
3. 15 minutes should be baked in a preheated oven. Dispatch the cake from the oven.
4. Mix the butter, milk, and caramels in a bowl that can be heated in a microwave. Stirring once or twice during the ten minutes on high will help the components melt and become smooth. The heated caramel mixture should be spread over the cake before the pecans and chocolate chips are added. Fill the remaining space with cake batter and spread it out.
5. Bake for 20 to 35 minutes in the preheated oven, or until the center of the cake springs back when lightly pressed.

Peach Cobbler

Serve: 1 |Time: 12 minutes

Cal| 512 Fat| 13.3 g Protein| 10 g Fiber| 9.6 g Cholesterol | 32 mg

Ingredients

- ❖ 15 g butter
- ❖ 30 g white sugar
- ❖ 30 g all-purpose flour
- ❖ 15g non-fat dry milk powder
- ❖ Pinch of baking powder
- ❖ Pinch of ground cinnamon
- ❖ 1 pinch of salt
- ❖ 30 ml water
- ❖ 110 g diced peaches, well-drained

Directions

1. Butter should be placed in a microwave-safe cup and heated on high for 20 seconds or until melted.
2. In a small bowl, combine the sugar, flour, milk powder, baking powder, cinnamon, and salt. Stir in the water. With a fork, pour the sugar mixture into the mug and whisk until the batter is thoroughly combined Peaches should be placed on top of the batter.
3. For two minutes, heat at 70% power in the microwave. Give the mug one more minute in the microwave. Cool a little.

Coffee Mug Cake

Serve: 1 |Time: 12 minutes

Cal| 507 Fat| 28.4 g Protein| 6.1 g Fiber| 2.1 g Cholesterol | 72 mg

Ingredients

- 15 g butter, softened
- 30 g white sugar
- ½ beaten egg
- 30 g sour cream
- 2 drops vanilla extract, or more to taste
- 32 g all-purpose flour
- Pinch of baking powder
- 30 g all-purpose flour
- 15 g brown sugar
- 4 g cinnamon
- 15 g butter

Directions

1. In a coffee cup, combine melted butter, and white sugar, and whisk until frothy. Add the egg, sour cream, and vanilla essence. Stir in 1/4 cup flour and baking powder while adding to the batter.
2. Brown sugar, cinnamon, and flour are combined in a bowl. Sprinkle the crumbly flour mixture over the mug of cake batter after using a fork or pastry cutter to blend in 1 tablespoon of butter.
3. Cook for one minute on high in the microwave. Cook for an additional 10 seconds at a time until a toothpick inserted in the center comes out clean.

Cake

Serve: 12 |Time: 10 minutes

Cal| 256 Fat| 6.2 g Protein| 3.4 g Fiber| 1.1 g Cholesterol | 42 mg

Ingredients

- ❖ 520 g package cake mix
- ❖ 3 eggs
- ❖ 600 g apple pie filling
- ❖ 120 g mashed banana

Directions

1. The cake mix should be completely blended with the pie filling, applesauce, eggs, and water until moist. As an alternative, use a dish with a microwave-safe cup or cone in the centre, or a Bundt pan (to mimic a Bundt pan). The mixture should be put in the bowl that holds the cup.
2. Bake for six minutes and thirty seconds on high, then turn the oven off and bake for another six minutes and thirty seconds. Remove the bowl from the oven, place a dish over it, and let it to stand for five minutes (this finishes the cooking process).
3. Turn the cake over onto a dish and take off the cone to create a deliciously quick dessert (cup). Serve hot with vanilla ice cream or whipped cream for the best results.

Chocolate Covered Blueberries

Serve: 36 |Time: 15 minutes

Cal| 39 Fat| 2 g Protein| 0.4 g Fiber| 0.2 g Cholesterol | 0 mg

Ingredients

- ❖ 210 g semi-sweet chocolate chips
- ❖ 15 g shortening
- ❖ 300 g fresh blueberries, rinsed and dried

Directions

1. Melt chocolate in a metal bowl over a pan of simmering water or in a microwave-safe glass bowl. Until melted and smooth, stirring often. The shortening should be added slowly while stirring until melted.
2. Using wax paper, cover a baking sheet.
3. Add blueberries and gently whisk to combine. Place small mounds of blueberries on the baking sheet that has been prepped.
4. For about 10 minutes, refrigerate until hard. Keep in an airtight container in a cool location. These should last for two days.

Conclusion

The microwave is now a necessary piece of equipment in every home. It enables you to cook food in addition to just heating it. If you have a new microwave and are unsure of how to use it best, you should be prepared with a few tips and techniques.

A magnetron, an electron rod, is what generates microwaves inside an oven. These waves travel quickly between the food and the metal oven walls before being absorbed by the food. The water molecules in the food vibrate as a result of these waves, creating heat.

Instead of gathering around a smoky fire to heat and reheat food, our forefathers would have adored a microwave. In the past ten years or so, microwaves have grown in popularity. They were heralded as the newest technological marvel and convenience for the home. The ability of microwaves to cook food indoors and outdoors without the use of a gas stove was one of their main selling points. Other considerations included conserving energy, immediate cooking, heating to your preference, and cooking whatever you desire. In the present era, microwaves are a common household item, but picking the proper one can be difficult. Do not fret! To determine which oven will meet your needs the best.

Printed in Great Britain
by Amazon

29289025R00066